GO
LiVE!

WILEY

Video and Virtual will shorten your time to success... sales success, life success, and legacy

Jeffrey Gitomer

King of Sales

The best time to
start a podcast
was 10 years ago.
The second
best time
is now.

Jeffrey Gitomer

King of Sales

GO LiVE!

TURN VIRTUAL CONNECTIONS INTO
PAYING CUSTOMERS

JEFFREY GITOMER

WILEY

Library of Congress Cataloging-in-Publication Data is available:

ISBN 9781119647133 (Hardcover)

ISBN 9781119647195 (ePDF)

ISBN 9781119647140 (ePub)

Editors: Jennifer Gluckow and Lisa Elmore

Page designer: Mike Wolff

Cover Design: Wiley
Cover Image: © Avector/Getty Images

Printed in the United States of America

SKY10021676_101220

FOREWORD

The Golden Ticket to Your Success!

You and I are living in a time in which innovation is your golden ticket to success. A time when technology creates opportunities, connections, and big booming businesses – born in even the smallest of towns. Your town?

I am speaking from personal experience. At the age of 18, I started my first business, which freed me from three retail jobs where I was working 90+ hours a week. It was enough to catch the entrepreneur bug and, while network marketing wasn't a final destination, I picked up the ability to learn and leverage social media and the internet to sell my product and myself.

Since then I have been down a few different paths to find my place as a digital marketer. Then I stumbled headfirst into podcasting. I knew I was home.

Instead of following the pack and doing what I had witnessed in the podcast industry, I asked myself… where is there room for innovation? Where can I make this an extremely effective space to prime, nurture, and connect with my audience to turn them into fiercely loyal buyers?

I questioned everything.
I evaluated everything.
I took action, and I started winning.

The online space and tools available to me as a marketer, even as a college dropout, allowed me to build a multi-six-figure business in just under a year. And to get the full picture, it was all from a spare guest room turned office, with a laptop that had far outlived its life, in a tiny town in Indiana. A town so small actually… my email list has more people.

And guess what? I'm not the exception anymore… I am the new rule.

The digital tools you have available as a business owner today are vast, far more superior, easier to use, and as life-changing for you as they were for me.

The live, digital, and virtual game is shifting, and you have an amazing and untapped opportunity to learn how to leverage your time, creativity, and services to make a difference – all while finding financial freedom for yourself, the same way I got mine.

The key is, and this is the tricky part, you have to love what you do, be willing to dive in deep, make mistakes, and learn as you go. There is no one better to teach you this than the King of Sales himself.

When I jumped on a Zoom call with Jeffrey and Jennifer, I am not going to lie, I was nervous. Sweaty palms and a few extra heartbeats while I was waiting to join the Zoom room.

I had performed an audit for their podcast, *Sell or Die,* and even though they had millions of downloads, successful businesses, and were best-selling authors, what I saw was extremely typical for the podcast industry.

It was identical to every single audit that had come before it, if I am being completely honest (and midwestern people are completely honest). A great podcast – but what was it doing in terms of building their business?

Pretty much nothing.

I am never sure how the initial response is going to go when I deliver the news, "Hey, we need to completely redo the entire way that you are using your podcast."

But Jeffrey and Jennifer Gitomer know the power of creativity and innovation.

They understand the power of questioning the status quo to find a better way, and then take action.

I remember days, even weeks later getting messages from them referencing what we worked through on that Zoom call still continuing to land. Big breakthroughs and shifts came through as we began our work together in this new direction, and continuing to work better week by week

It's hard to think that the whole live, virtual, and podcast industry is doing things wrong. You watch your mentors, the people you look up to, and all the other people around you running a webinar or launching a podcast the same way. You think, "This must be how it's done. This is what breeds success in the online space. Then you just start plugging away replicating the steps they took." Eh, not quite.

This is the case with anything in business, isn't it?

You watch and mimic. You follow those with status, blue checkmarks, and book deals. Virtual and podcast must be the same, right? Right?

I'm challenging you to look through a different lens and to clearly define what virtual success means to you. In the online world of sales, I want you to ditch the notion that popularity = success.

My husband and I have two girls, 3 and 5. When we talk about what our role is in their lives as parents, what our deepest desires are for them, it always comes down to the same thing: "Happy, healthy, and successful in their *own* definition."

Those definitions cannot come from us; they have to come from them. Just like your definition has to come from you. We can guide our children, but ultimately their success and happiness must come from their own choices.

What does success look like for *you*? What is *your* definition of success? Certainly not the same as everyone else's.

My guess is that your definition has more to do with the impact you have on people, the lifestyle you live or seek to live, and the absence of a semi–panic attack every time you log into your bank account.

If I had to also guess, I would say that the number of followers, video views, or comments on your Instagram posts didn't make it into that definition. When you focus on connections, mastering digital marketing, impact-driven sales, and innovation, those numbers don't matter.

Popularity does not = success. Always remember that.

Jeffery is going to teach you how to be the new rule in a world that has evolved more quickly than anyone could have imagined.

Master the concepts he shares in this book and you will be able to harness the power of social media, video, and podcasts to sell from anywhere, regardless of the number of followers you have.

It's time to *Go Live!* with your vision, and claim your version of virtual success.

Tara Counterman

Tara Counterman
Founder of Profitable Podcast Productions

PREFACE
Here's what's in this book...

The Power of Understanding through
audible and visible clarity.

SEE ME – VIDEO – HEAR ME! Who? YOU!
Tell me, talk to me. Don't send text to me.
Understand me better by listening
to my tone and hearing and or
watching my emotions.

The cost of misinterpreting a text message
or a message sent in text by email.

The power of broadcasting emotionally
and being understood, agreed with,
believed, and trusted.

The power of podcasting. Having
your own show with unlimited
Marketing AND Sales value.

Profitability Secrets and our two million
download *Sell or Die* podcast broken down
to easily understand and implement.

The sales and monetary value of going LIVE.

The sales value and strategies of virtual.

The sales value and strategies of video.

Your next 10 years of emerging sales strategies…

2020-2030 is Your Time

The ONE WORD…

When I say, "video," what one word comes to mind?

When I say, "Make your own video," what one word comes to mind?

When I say, "Make your own video and send it to a customer to try to make a connection or a sale?" what one word comes to mind?

When I say, "virtual meeting," what one word comes to mind?

When I say, "virtual sales call," what one word comes to mind?

When I say, "Zoom coffee meeting with the prospect or customer," what one word comes to mind?

When I say, "Start your podcast," what one word comes to mind?

When I say, "Have a Facebook Live every week," what one word comes to mind?

When I say, "Start your YouTube channel," what one word comes to mind?

When I say, "Do a daily Instagram Story," what one word comes to mind?

When I say, "Embed a video in all your sales emails," what one word comes to mind?

When I say, "Add a video to all your LinkedIn communications," what one word comes to mind?

The word is NOW! If you want two words they would be... RIGHT NOW!

BUT if I ask you, "How is your virtual and video prowess?" your answer would be... "not right now!"

Jeffrey Gitomer
King of Sales

P.S. Check your calendar…
This book was written in 2020 for the next decade, not 6 months following the global pandemic. The dates may vary – the principles of new connecting, presenting, and selling strategies will not.

Live, Virtual, Video, Distance Presenting, Distance Learning, and Distance Selling are here for at least the next decade and will intensify as years pass.

Jeffrey Gitomer

CONTENTS

THINK ABOUT THIS:

When a prospect or customer visits your website...

What do you want them to think?

What are they thinking now?

What do you want them to say?

What are they saying now?

What do you want them to do?

What are they doing now?

Now do something about it!

Jeffrey Gitomer

We are entering a new era. Are you in?

The post-pandemic productivity and profit plan process or, simply stated, the New Normal, is about your new and personal messaging and ability to connect with customers and prospects.

A new way. A video way. A podcast way. A virtual way. A live way. A broadcast way.

This New Normal will affect your personal productivity, your ability to do your personal best, display your personal integrity, communicate with your positive projection, prove your ability to adapt to the recovering economy, and prove your ability to adapt to the recovering customer.

Taking the virtual and live path will position you as a leader. It will help you perform like and be perceived as a winner. It will project your positive attitude, your communication skills, your knowledge, your self-confidence, and the depth of your belief. And of course, you'll make more sales – lots more sales.

GOT BALLS? You're in luck! At this time in our business history, it's a great opportunity (maybe the best opportunity ever) for you to try something new, reinvent your sales process, pivot a business, start a business, or take action on an idea, and emerge as a winner.

What exactly is the New Normal? Where will it go? When will it end? Well, nobody knows for sure, but live, virtual, and video are at the core, and they are going to last a generation.

Live, video, and virtual have already challenged you to master new skills heretofore not seen as absolute or imperative before the pandemic…, but they are now. And these new skills will change you to be a better salesperson, leader, and/or entrepreneur.

And in case you're wondering, wandering, or waiting for things to "go back to the way they were," that's never going to happen.

Video, virtual, creativity, distance sales calls, in home studio, are new approaches to engaging while selling to new and existing customers. And it's not going away. It's going to bring to light your true technological prowess, the depth of your existing relationships, and your ability to adjust to emerging situations and new technologies and, of course, your rededication to personal attitude and personal excellence.

Jeffrey Gitomer

In other words... Get with Live, Virtual, and Video now, master it now, or lose to someone who has, whether the date is 2020 or 2030.

Jeffrey Gitomer

Go Live…
requires a new level of understanding about how the sales world, and your sales world, will move forward.

This is a book of ideas, strategies, explanations, and answers that require actions. And your results will be based on your YES attitude, your level of desire, your personal ambition, your mental determination, and your dedication to excellence.

Jeffrey Gitomer

Is Your Picture in Focus?

"In times of uncertainty, document what you are certain of." That gold nugget was casually passed on to me on our *Sell or Die* podcast by our guest and futurist Daniel Burrus. Boom.

Think about your certainties...

The one element that you're totally certain of and in total control of is YOU. After that there are five elements somewhat under your control and influence that will have an impact on your outcomes – based on your words and your actions. You can influence and impact your family, your friends, your business, your customers, and your social footprint.

I want you to document all the things that you're certain about yourself. What do you know to be true about your capabilities, your assets? What do you know to be true about your customers right now? What do you know to be true about the things that you can control about yourself, what you're willing to dedicate (and invest) the time to read more about, to learn more about video, document the things you're certain about yourself: your assets, your expertise, all the things that you know about you.

Then document all the things that you're certain of about your family, your friends, your circle of influence, your business, your customers, and your social network. Just take a few moments and document the things that you know to be true about all of those elements.

You're in control of you, and that's good news. This is going to save you hours, maybe days of looking to control other people and other things you can influence. You can impact, but you cannot control. So I want you to take a moment, or a few moments, put this book down, and document your certainties in a Google Doc or Word file.

- Your best qualities
- Your assets
- Your skills
- Your achievements
- Your expertise
- Your attraction
- Your reputation
- Your passions
- Your desires
- Your near-term goals
- Your present situation
- Your needs as a parent
- Your needs in a career
- Your needs in life
- Your virtual prowess (rate 1–10)
- Your social footprint (rate 1–10)
- Your ability to make a video (rate 1–10)
- Your personal brand (rate 1–10)

This self-analysis gives you an "accurate" picture of YOU – or should I say, as accurate as you're willing to be with yourself.

Now that you have defined your personal certainties, it's going to be a hell of a lot easier to define your other certainties...

- Your family
- Your friends and close people
- Your business – co-workers – your assets – your needs
- The state of your business and your market as you know it right now
- Your customers – their recent stories – their immediate needs
- The state of their business and the present state of their market

You now have clear vision and a solid understanding of your total present situation. That was (not so) easy.

Reluctant
GO LIVE Warrior

goes from nervous, self-conscious and unprepared to GO LIVE and emerges as self-confident, enthusiastic, world-class

You're reading this book on going live, which means you know you need to do more live streaming to grow your business. The fact is, you can have all the strategies in the world, but if you have a fear of going live (like I did), then you need to read this chapter before you keep going. Because the strategies you're about to learn are gold if, and only if, you put them into practice.

I remember when I was about four years old and my dad took me to *Sesame Street Live* so that I could be on TV. Up until this day, I don't remember my dad ever taking a day off, so even at four, I knew this was huge #nopressure. The minute we arrived at that grand, fancy building in NYC, I froze. I wouldn't go on the set. I was terrified. My stage fright was bigger than Big Bird. My dad even promised me a candy bar after I went on the set, but I never mustered up the courage to go on TV (and I never got that candy bar).

I learned a great lesson. When you don't go live, you miss out on the candy bar. Okay, okay, all joking aside. The opportunity is on the other side of the live – the minute you press that "go live" button, you are creating opportunity – business opportunity, personal opportunity, brand-building opportunity, social media opportunity, connection opportunity, growth opportunity, revenue opportunity, and partnership opportunity. WOW!

They say the universe continues to give you the lessons you need until you receive them. (I don't know who the "they" is.) When I started my business, I knew it was imperative to create videos and go live, however, that same reluctance, fear and nervousness set in. Like you, I had a desire to do it, but the fear factor was overwhelming. Finally, I came to the conclusion that to win in my business, my desire needed to be greater than my fear.

Every time I made a video or went live I asked self-defeating questions like: What if no one shows up? What should I talk about? What if I mess up? Who am I to teach these things? Some other expert already speaks about this, why would anyone want to hear about it from me? Suppose someone asks me a question that I can't answer? Ever ask yourself any of those questions?

Those kinds of questions stem from limiting beliefs – beliefs that are preventing you from taking the kind of action you and your customers deserve. Beliefs that will prevent you from growing your business, your sales, your success, and your fun factor. Limiting beliefs often stem from situations that occurred in your childhood (aka *Sesame Street Live* for me) and you may not even realize you're carrying them with you – usually they're hidden and they seem so real that they feel like facts instead of beliefs.

To overcome them, you first need to identify the beliefs that exist and search for the truth or alternate meanings. My stage fright came from a young age, and when I was able to go back in my timeline and identify the exact moment it started and relate to the fears I had as that four-year-old, I could overcome them as an adult. Imagine your timeline. What situations have you experienced that may be contributing to your current belief system? Where did your fear begin? Think about it. Was there a time you decided your voice wasn't as important as it should be?

To inject more positive, result-oriented beliefs, you can begin to ask yourself better questions like: Instead of asking who are you to go live, you should be asking, why not you?! What kind of knowledge and expertise do you possess that you could share? What are the consequences of holding back that information? Think both consequences to yourself and your business and to your clients and prospects. What kind of evidence can you find when you tried something new and it was difficult the first time, but after practice it got easier and easier – like riding a bike. Each time you fall, you get right back up.

With the support of my husband (confession: The author of this book) and an amazing team, I pushed through my fears and went live. And I will be the first to say, my first few videos sucked, just like my first couple of blog posts. The good news is, they got easier and better over time with practice and self-coaching. I painfully watched my own performances and took notes.

Think back to that question from earlier: What if no one shows up to your live video? Imagine that no one showing up is actually a great opportunity – an opportunity for you to practice and get comfortable with how to go live, with your style, with the technology. What if you could believe that everything that happened with your life is always working in your favor?

After creating hundreds of videos and attracting thousands of subscribers, I discovered the secret sauce to going live. I call it the CANDY BAR Method because going live should be layered with sweet opportunity rewards.

The CANDY BAR Method: Create – Attract – Narrate – Debrief – Your Opportunity Belief Attitude Repetition

Create. This is the part where a lot of people get stuck – how to create a description that will stop the scroll, what to say when you're live, what to do if you don't know an answer. It's time to get out of your head and into your customer's head – What does your customer need?

Attract. Use my *Three-Part Attraction Formula:* 1. Offer content that people will WANT to share. 2. Ask your viewers to invite or share with others. 3. Thank them for sharing.

Narrate. Script and spontaneous. Make sure you don't look like or sound like you're reading. You can practice and record on your screen or your phone to see what it looks like. What is the outcome you want your viewers to have? Start with the end in mind and build your content plan around the actions you want your customers to take.

Debrief. 1. Watch your videos. 2. Make popcorn and be ready to be vulnerable. 3. Coach yourself and be coachable. Watch your videos, take note, and create action items for improvement, take action and repeat. You will be raising the bar each time. In addition to self-coaching, find people you trust and get their feedback. Our former producer, Doug, used to give me real, unbiased, positive, spirited feedback that would help me improve. Who's your Doug?

Your Opportunity. YES!!! This is what it's all about. Check in with yourself – What's your ROV? Return on Video? Your business opportunity, your connection opportunity, your growth opportunity, your partnership opportunity, and of course, your revenue opportunity.

Belief. Your thoughts determine your actions and your actions determine your results. It's that simple. When you believe you CAN go live, that you can be great at going live, that you can attract and impact lots of people by going live, that you can create community by going live and that you can create revenue by going live, then you WILL achieve those things. *Ask yourself:* Are my current beliefs helping me or hurting me?

Attitude. Your energy and attitude are contagious even, or especially through the computer screen. And it starts with personal determination and pride in what you do. Your audience will pick up on your attitude, and if you ever wonder if you're bringing a good attitude, just check your audience because your vibe attracts your tribe. My audience is filled with can-do, high-energy, YES! entrepreneurs and salespeople. Yours?

Repetition. You WILL get great at going live, but it may not happen as you expect it to, in a New York minute. Just like eating an apple a day to keep the doctor away, it will happen slowly over time, day-by-day, as you take consistent improvement action.

Your turn to step up to the bar (the candy bar!). "Say what? It can't be that easy, Jen." Oh yes, yes it can. It's like jumping into the deep end without floaties on before you know how to swim. You'll survive. When you take that leap of faith in yourself, your video equivalent to the doggy paddle will kick in and eventually you'll be floating on your back with sheer confidence.

If you're still resistant to going live, then I need to bring my New York out and tell you this straight up: Not going live is selfish. Holding back your information, your knowledge, your strategies that can help someone be successful cause you're too afraid you may not be good enough is selfish. Stop focusing on yourself and start focusing on your customer.

Once you overcome your resistance to going live, with practice and repetition, you gain self-confidence, experience, a new enthusiasm for what you're conveying, what you're selling, build a strong community, and connect with people on a deeper level.

Here's to you "going live" and giving yourself your own candy bar – and the sweetness of new opportunity (real sugar only please, none of that Splenda stuff).

Jen Gitomer

Jen Gitomer

Now that you have a clear vision of your total picture, you can begin to document the opportunities that your clear vision has uncovered and create your own plan of action that includes your ideas, objectives, intentions, and wisdom.

Jeffrey Gitomer

YOUR
9.5
GO LIVE
CHALLENGES

1

MASTER THE NEW VOICE, LANGUAGE, CONTENT, AND STRATEGY OF SALES AND SELLING

The past pandemic has restructured the sales and selling process – and it's never going back. All aspects of sales and selling will have a GO LIVE element, and your even-the-playing-field opportunity is to master every element.

START HERE: in order to master the new voice, the new language, the new content, and strategy of sales and selling, it's going to take an open mind and a rededication to your personal development.

You can't develop as a salesperson until you develop as a person.

It's going to be a softer sell for a few years. You're going to have to use an empathetic voice and have an understanding heart – even if you live in NYC.

You're going to **help customers first**. You're going to help customers win. You're going to have enthusiasm and encouragement for the customer. You're going to have to have **winning ideas in favor of the customer**, rather than a bunch of slides and a "sales presentation."

You're going to need, create, and present a **value-based message** in terms of the customer – **bringing an idea** to establish a creative advantage.

STRATEGY: Few or no slides. Whoa. And the secret sauce is to **create a competitive advantage** with undeniable perceived value, and sell to help. **Help customers win.** Here's the deal.

In this new emerging economy, whatever you want to call it, I'm calling it the New Normal, you're going to be exposed for who you are and who you are not based on what you've done, the actions you've taken, the questions you ask, your perceived motive, and the way you present yourself – virtually.

How ready are you for the new virtual and online-in-person customer?

Let me get a little bit more detailed. Your new voice has to be empathetic, softer, trustworthy, informative, helpful, and encouraging.

HERE'S THE CLUE: The new presentation begins by asking people for their stories – What has happened in people's business or career, how were they impacted by COVID-19 or lockdown, and while you're asking for their stories, you're going to take notes… notes to yourself about the story, ideas about how you can help, trends you're noticing and how you can comfortably offer help. In short, opportunities.

HERE'S THE KEY: Try to relate to others without being maudlin, but still be both empathetic and sympathetic. Make certain that any offer to help is in terms of the other person, not you. Don't tell people how they're going to save money. I want you to talk about positive and profitable outcomes and profitable incomes, whether it pertains to you and your business or not. GENUINE HELP.

NOTE WELL: If customers are willing to share their stories and their needs, and you have an idea about how you can help, you have established a competitive advantage. In their minds, you're genuine. Meanwhile, your competitors are going to be out there plotting how to make more sales and make their quota. BIG MISTAKE. They're going to try to bring their slide deck.

CLUE: Throw your slide deck away. Bring an idea of value based on the story that customers have told you. Customers are in scramble mode. They have no time and no patience for a slide deck or a sales pitch "at your lowest prices ever."

Give me a break.

BUT everyone has time for help and an idea. EVERYONE.

TIME OUT: I want you to create one idea each **right now** for at least three customers before moving on to the next lesson.

THINK: What can you offer to or give to each customer that they will perceive as valuable?

MAJOR CLUE: The value must be perceived or an offer has no value.

Throw away your worthless "value prop" and substitute a value offer or a value statement or a valuable idea. Create something of value for your customers before you move on to the next lesson. It has to have perceived value and shows customers how they win.

HELP CUSTOMERS WIN, AND YOU WIN.
You win their hearts and minds first, and eventually, when THEIR time is right, you will win the order. I promise.

Jeffrey Gitomer

Read it. Think about it.

ACT ON IT!

At the end of each of the 9.5 Challenges of GO LIVE, you will find a TAKE ACTION page with specific decisions you must make, ideas you must implement, and winning strategies you can put into action to maximize the value of this book and your virtual and live reality success.

FIRST CHALLENGE ACTION –

- **Don't read this book – STUDY IT – Harvey Mackay's most powerful quote**
- **Decide you are willing to take a leadership position**
- **Make a game plan to HELP before you make a game plan to SELL**
- **Post-it Note your intentions on your bathroom mirror**
- **Don't just set new goals – set new standards**

Start NOW!...

CHALLENGE 1 ACTIONS

MASTER THE NEW VOICE, LANGUAGE, CONTENT, AND STRATEGY OF SALES AND SELLING.

- Help BEFORE you sell – THE WINNING LIVE STRATEGY.
- Find and document their stories and their needs FIRST.
- Take time to understand them and their situation BEFORE YOU OFFER ANY ANSWERS.
- Decide you will NOT sell until THEY ARE READY TO BUY!
- Substitute your slide deck for a human conversation.
- Start slow and soft until you feel it's time to speed up.
- Make sure to offer ideas that help THEM.
- TAKE ACTION.

2

MASTER VIRTUAL

During the stay-at-home pandemic, your world became virtual. And in case you hadn't noticed, it has stayed that way, never to return to the old way. And it's a better way.

Odds are while you were at home, you had more virtual meetings of some kind in 60 days than you had in your entire life. And it's going to stay that way. From this day forward, half of your meetings, or more, are going to take place virtually.

Less will be more… and less will be less…
Less "going to the office" = less commute time = more time to be productive.
Fewer face-to-face meetings = more virtual = less travel = more selling time.
Less destination air travel = more opportunity to be creative = more selling time.

SURROUND YOURSELF WITH A FIRST-CLASS LOOK

The VIRTUAL question is:
Have you mastered your virtual opportunity
or are you just turning on your computer,
making sure it works, and sitting in
front of your closet door
or in your poorly lit office?

What is the impression you're projecting BEFORE you say a word?

- **Do you look great to your customer on the other end?**
- **What are your visible surroundings?**
- **If you need a backdrop beyond your closet or office, go here: UseAnyVoo.com and get a personal or corporate branded screen.**
- **How's your lighting? Do you look bright or dark?**
- **Have you bought a video light or a ring light? When you face people, you have to look bright and alive. NOT AN OPTION to ignore appearances.**
- **How do you sound? GET A REAL MICROPHONE – lose your earbuds.**
- **How's your technology?**
- **Have your look and tech mastered BEFORE you make a call.**

Once all of these virtual elements are in place, then you have to slowly, slowly, slowly master the process. Why is this an imperative? Because virtual meetings and virtual selling and video broadcasting will be a way of life for the foreseeable future.

You have to be prepared to make a presentation, or any type of sales or business call, from any place virtually and on video.

Jeffrey Gitomer

REALITY: Virtual has become the New Normal. Being able to sell live without being there, yet being able to make them feel your presence, your professionalism, your emotion, your sincerity, your value, your self-confidence, your believability, and your trustworthiness.

Many people don't feel comfortable yet in front of the camera. You have to be. You have to look relaxed and in control. You have to look ready to be a friend, and you have to come through with a self-assured essence and a trustworthiness that people will pick up on, and ultimately make them want to buy from you.

THE VALUE AND REALITY OF YOUR "SELLING TIME"

Think about this: Let's suppose you live in Columbus, Ohio, it's March 2019, and you "have" to go to Dallas, Texas, for a meeting. It's a sales meeting. And you get to the airport at 6:00 in the morning, and the plane's a little delayed. You don't actually get on the plane till 8:30 or 9:00. You get to Dallas at 11:30 a.m. You get to the customer's place by 12 o'clock. You have lunch with them, and then you have your two-hour meeting, and they love you, and they tell you to send them a proposal. You make a few business sales calls and whatever until you have dinner at 6:00 p.m. Dinner is over at 8:00 p.m., and you go back to the airport if there's a flight or stay overnight. Whatever time you get home, you're shot.

Cost? You don't want to know. Plus loss of real productivity.

NOW THINK ABOUT THIS:

Same scenario, September 2020. You could have had that same meeting *virtually* at seven or eight o'clock in the morning from your bedroom. No airport. No flight. Sent their favorite K-cups in advance and a signed book from their favorite author (me?). You could have talked for an hour or two, made your presentation, sent a video proposal, and closed the deal. Then at nine o'clock met with somebody else, and then at ten o'clock somebody else, and at 11 o'clock met with somebody else, and at noon had a virtual lunch with somebody else. Get it?

What is your (selling) time worth?

How are you investing your time to make more of it? More meetings, more presentations, more personal relationships, and of course – more sales.

HINT: more virtual!

THINK. And rethink. Do you think corporations will fly people to Dallas for one meeting? Well, maybe they will if it's to close or save a deal. So let's say they cut that budget in half. Let's say half the meetings you're going to fly to or drive to, but the other half you can conduct in your own home – or maybe in your office. But either way, it's going to be virtual and your customers will love it, because they don't have to deal with getting ready for you.

Want more sales/coffee meetings? Bring your own coffee, send them coffee, send them some Death Wish Coffee or a box of their favorite K-cups, or a Starbucks gift card so you can have coffee with them. Same with lunch.

Virtual is the new way to meet, BUT you have to be creatively prepared for it. You have to have a success look, and take creative-success actions. All you have to do is look professional, be enthusiastic about the message that you convey, and add the element of creative surprise.

WAKE UP AND SMELL THE SALES: You can't look like you just got out of bed. The best thing you can do when you get out of bed in the morning is make it, and go with an AnyVoo as a background. You can put that AnyVoo anyplace, and look like you have your professional brand together.

Let me show you mine. This is my AnyVoo, (UseAnyVoo.com). And this can be your virtual sales call or meeting background. This can be in front of your bed that's not made and you still look professional – for less than the cost of a one-way airplane ticket.

The room

The view

Now you still have to be ready to make the sales call. But if you're going to have a virtual office, you might as well make it look great.

Now, the challenge for you, and this is a huge challenge, is to MASTER every strategy I share, the strategies and the assets that you're going to need to be able to make sales happen in your home or virtually. But it's your responsibility to gather the resources, master them, and use them when you… Go Live.

The virtual sales call is your new ticket to increased revenue and increased ability to build relationships with people you don't shake hands with, but you CAN impact just the same.

They can be anywhere in the world or they can be five blocks away, but wherever they are, virtual is going to be a big portion of your new sales process, and the only way you're going to master it is by doing it, and then doing it again, and then doing it again, and then doing it again.

HINT: Watch your own videos. Do you love them every time you see them? This is your virtual record. YOU MUST WATCH yourself every single time you record.

Then ask yourself this painful question, "Would you buy from you?" I wonder whether you would or not.

VIDEO VIRTUAL SUCCESS CHALLENGE:
Record virtual meetings
until you love them,
and you love yourself,
and you feel as though your
message is being emotionally
transferred to people who
can say yes to you.
**That's the secret of video and
virtual success.**

Jeffrey Gitomer

It's a new sales world. It's a New Normal. Get in it now. Jumping in now so that you can emerge as a leader, not a lagger. Be ready. The world has changed. The world is continuing to change with new opportunities. Take advantage of the opportunities that are within your grasp, or lose to someone who takes them away.

You can't ignore virtual. It has become, and is going to be, the "new way" to sell for a long time to come. Be the master.

My GO LIVE can be your GO LIVE

On March 16, 2020, I began my journey into daily Facebook Live.

Like all new endeavors, it started slowly. A dozen or so participants in 100 or so views. But as COVID became more of an issue, I decided to take a more strategic and specific role in my daily show. I added insight and inspiration for those who were struggling, and sure enough the audience grew. Rapidly. Daily. Momentum built.

I began to recognize that not only was there a need, but there was a virtual outcry for help. And as the audience grew, and many were there daily, they began to interact with one another. Not just on the live broadcast but also meeting later, forming groups, doing chats, doing their own live shows. It was a phenomenon.

Every morning at 9:59 a.m. Seven days a week. Never missing a day regardless of the circumstances. Traveling, internet outages, scrambling for venues, nothing got in my way. If you're reading this in 2021, I'm still doing it. As of January 1, 2021, I will have been live 291 straight days and counting. Every day at 9:59 a.m. on my Facebook public page – Facebook.com/JeffreyGitomer. Join me and let me know you're reading the book.

I decided to launch a course called "The New Normal." I had people go on a waiting list. They did. Hundreds of people signed up. I made it very affordable for those who are struggling. I included a Facebook community page that went nuts with activity and value.

Along the way I took the advice of Ken Walls and went from Facebook to StreamYard as my broadcasting platform (useStreamyard.live).

StreamYard allowed me to add all of my social media platforms together in one broadcast. My audience immediately doubled. I was able to combine Facebook, all my private Facebook groups, YouTube, and Twitter.

Here are the Learnings of Live and the Virtues of Virtual details that I discovered, delivered, implemented, and banked – and so can you...

- **Consistency of date and time.** If you don't go daily, make sure it's weekly at the same day and time. I HAVE ESTABLISHED A LEADERSHIP POSITION. If the show is compelling, people will share, tell others, and show up regularly.

- **My key to GO LIVE success is a Daily Value Message on Facebook – I select a topic and create a title.** The principle is simple (but not easy) I ENGAGE WITH VALUABLE CONTENT DAILY. An uplifting message that is immediately implementable. A combination of hope and applicable content.

- **I am on Facebook, BUT I don't use Facebook to broadcast.**

- **I use StreamYard to broadcast (UseStreamYard.live) –** I can combine all my social platforms and groups onto one stream – and I can show slides, run a title message across the bottom of my screen, and add a guest on StreamYard with ease. Call it Power Live Broadcasting.

- **Engaging people who attend, and including them in the broadcast is imperative.**

- **People are grateful for the messages and the consistency, and tell me so every day.**

- **Because of my value offered, people are more than willing to buy from me.**

- **People greet, engage, befriend, and buy from each other.**

- **Deals are made – I have made several.** Most notably with Justin Benton at 101CBD.org. We're coming out with a powerful CBG oil ahead of the marketing curve.

- **Amazing people show up and contribute – Pat Hazell – Steve Rizzo – Joe Soto – surprises.**

- **"Voice of Customer" rings out, and unsolicited testimonials reign and rain.**

- **My group has spawned other groups – they take deep dives into subjects discussed.**

- **And I got instant response and acceptance to real world, helpful ideas.**

- **I am able to customize my message for the moment, and give timely help.**

- **It's genuinely interactive – I give 100 shout-outs a day, ask for opinions, ideas, and positive things.**

- **People fight to be FIRST ON.**

- **Virality by sharing.** I ask for participants to share the broadcast to their connections and they do. Gladly.

- **I have created a Community, not formed a business group.**

My daily live show woke me up by waking them up. I gave clarity and I GOT clarity.

Author's Note – Literally, as I was writing this passage, my lifelong friend, comedian, speaker, and author Steve Rizzo called. He's a frequent visitor to my morning Facebook Live show. Out of the blue he started talking about the live show. He said, "You know, something has changed in you. Ever since you started your morning show you have become an even MORE GIVING person. The show is informal, informative, inspirational intentional, and interactive – Jeffrey, it's way beyond motivation – people feel involved and are eager to participate – I love how they race to be first on." I smiled and felt an ounce of humility and a pound of gratefulness that my mission (help other people) was understood by my close friend – and hopefully by you.

How Going LIVE Creates a Revenue Generating Ripple Effect in Your Business

By Joe Soto

Since 2010 I've been showing up online via video. I started creating YouTube videos that year and haven't stopped since. Video was and still is the game changer if you embrace it and are willing to consistently put out valuable content to an audience that is hungry for it.

But nothing compares to the power of going LIVE on video to your audience.

In 2017 I decided to create an online program called Marketing Agency Academy, specifically designed to help digital marketing consultants and agency owners start and grow their business to seven-figures in sales revenue.

I recorded over 100 video lessons for the course and launched it for $997.

The course generated over $750,000 in revenue and is still selling today.

Here's an interesting fact: **I recorded the entire course in my basement, using my iPhone and a $20 tripod** I purchased from Amazon.

I did the same thing with my second online course release, a program called Funnel Sales Academy, which has generated an additional half million dollars in sales.

This course was also recorded using my iPhone and, for a few screenshare lessons, my laptop.

The most important decision I made when I started selling my program was creating a private Facebook group just for students of my courses.

Why was this decision so important? **Because of the ripple effect it can create in your business.**

Going LIVE gave me a platform to give more value and serve at a more intimate level. Because it gave me the platform to GO LIVE in the Facebook group every week for group Q & A, allowing me to address my students concerns in an exclusive LIVE online setting.

Going LIVE every week bonded me to my students. They can see, hear, and feel my emotions when I'm on a Facebook LIVE with them, addressing their toughest challenges as they come up. I demonstrated I was committed to their success *just by showing up every week* on the Facebook Live Q&A sessions.

Going LIVE helped me sell more courses. When selling my course, I highlight that I'll be there for them each week with "LIVE" coaching and Q&A via Facebook Live. This helps me sell more courses for three reasons, 1) they can anticipate me helping them if they need help beyond the lessons, 2) it differentiates me from most others who are selling similar online programs who aren't willing to put forth the effort to go LIVE each week, and 3) when it comes time to launch a new course, they are trusting, eager buyers.

Going LIVE helped me sell out my in-person event. When it came time to announce my first LIVE, in-person, three-day weekend event I filled all the seats within the first two weeks of announcing it. I had dozens of students confirm that the weekly Facebook Lives contributed to their quick decisions to sign-up and attend the event. Many of these people traveled from as far as Australia and Singapore to Washington, D.C., where I held the event, just to meet me in person *because they felt they already knew me.*

Going LIVE gave me a platform to give more value and serve at a more intimate level. Because it gave me the platform to GO LIVE in the Facebook Group every week for group Q &A, allowing me to address my students concerns in an exclusive LIVE Online setting.

Joe Soto

Because of this bond, it made it easy for me to offer and sell out my year-long mastermind program for a premium fee.

Going LIVE can help *you* do all these things too.

What's even more interesting is that I've done all this and more with nine kids, seven of them still in the home, all under the age of 15 while creating these courses.

My wife and I are blessed, but as you can imagine distractions in our home are inevitable.

I marvel at my kids impeccable timing. For example, on numerous occasions my four-year-old would decide to use the bathroom closest to my home office, then flush the toilet while proudly announcing to the house, "I pooped," while I was LIVE on Facebook with my group!

Sometimes the kids would decide to play (or yell) outside of my home office, or even charge into my office and jump onto my lap to wave to my students.

Distractions are going to happen. Deal with it and GO LIVE anyway. People will relate more to you when you're authentic and show up as you.

Lastly, if you're going to GO LIVE, you might as well make it count. Going LIVE on your Facebook, Instagram, LinkedIn or YouTube account can go to waste if nobody knows you doing it. Here are some of my favorite promotion tips:

- **Poll your Facebook friends or fans, asking them the most pressing question or challenge they face around your topic.** This creates engagement and opens the door for you to announce ahead of time that you'll be GOING LIVE to share your best ideas and tips.

- **Create an Event on your Facebook page announcing that you'll be going LIVE so people are notified ahead of time.**

- **Email your list (If you don't have one, start building one), let them know the details of when and where you'll be GOING LIVE.**
- **Advertise it on FB to your intended audience.** While this is more advanced, you can learn to do this at https://www.facebook.com/business. You can advertise it after you've gone live and people can watch the archive.

As Jeffrey Gitomer has pointed out, people don't buy your words as much as they buy you. My hope for you is you're inspired to take action using the principles and strategies you've learned in this book to create your own ripple effect in your business.

Joe Soto

CHALLENGE 2
ACTIONS

MASTER VIRTUAL.

- Rate yourself on a scale of 1 to 5 for each virtual element.
- Create your personal virtual space.
- Practice by DOING one meeting a day. Record it. Watch it. Improve it!
- Document your progress and celebrate sales and successes.
- Get feedback from people you know, love, and trust, but understand that YOU are your best judge and critic.
- Study and implement Joe Soto's ideas. He is brilliant, and his ideas work.
- These initial actions are critical to your overall success.
- Consistency wins.

3
MASTER VIDEO

Video has become your go-to communication method and strategy, and you may not have had a choice. If it's going to be an integral part of your communications and sales, you'd better master it.

I intend to make video my primary method of communication in all that I do and convey. I'm going to invest a few pages here talking to you about how to shoot a video and what to say in your video.

CHOICE: You have three video choices:

1. **You can reluctantly go into this, or**
2. **You can enthusiastically go into this, or**
3. **You can ignore this opportunity.**

NOTE: Don't start out by worrying about what your hair looks like, although you have to be presentable, concentrate on your message and your passion.

WHEN YOU START TO RECORD: Have something compelling to say. State it with deep belief and conviction. Smile when you talk. Look up, look people in the eye. Even if you don't have any hair, you have to look nice. You have to have good lighting. You have to have a good camera. You have to have a good microphone. You have to have a venue that's both comfortable and inviting. You have to sound enthusiastic. You have to sound credible. You have to sound self-assured and self-confident. In short, the Boy Scout motto prevails: BE PREPARED. Followed closely by the Dale Carnegie success mantra: BE YOURSELF.

If all of that works, you must first test-record what you plan to say before you ever say it, live or recorded, to send to a customer. You can just go into Zoom or QuickTime and record yourself, watch the video, and see how you like it. If you don't like it, that's you! Fix it, re-record it, because your customers are going to look at the same damn thing, and they're going to make a determination whether they're going to buy from you or not.

Based on you watching your own video, ask yourself:

- **How enthusiastic were you?**
- **How sincere were you?**
- **How clear is your message?**
- **How compelling were you?**
- **What does the background look like?**

All the elements that go into a video recording have to be in harmony to achieve customer acceptability (the only acceptability that matters).

ASK YOURSELF THIS OUCH QUESTION: Am I acceptable right now to the person I'm talking to, and will they buy from me as a result of this message?

That's huge.

STUDIO YOU!

Let's take a moment to discuss "venue" options.

My venue is my library. I've chosen this as my venue, because I have four or five areas that I can just flip the lights and camera on and it's kind of cool. Books make me/you look intelligent.

You can either be standing or sitting, but I think you should stand. You can sit, but it's just not quite as enthusiastic. You can't quite get your message out there as well when you're sitting as you can when you're standing.

When you're standing, you project yourself on the video so that the customer is buying you, and your persona, and your enthusiasm, and your sincerity, and your self-confidence, and I don't know that you can exude that same charisma as well from a chair.

I just don't think you match that emotion sitting in a chair or behind a desk, unless you have a professional setting and a professional crew. BUT SITTING IS OK. In the end, it's all about how you look, how you sound, how you project yourself, and, of course, the perceived value of your message. I shoot on both a camera and my laptop. And I shoot BOTH sitting and standing.

To practice you can shoot video on your laptop facing into you. Just hit "record" on any of a number of programs and you'll start to see yourself, and be able to coach yourself right away. It's not that difficult to start or do, but it is difficult to master. You will evolve slowly. Take small steps on a day-by-day basis. You must watch yourself to see what you look like, to hear what you sound like, and to dissect your message – because that's what your customers are looking at, that's what your customers are listening to, and they're going to make a buying decision based on that.

NOTE WELL: Customers and prospects will want to connect with you virtually and, when they do, they want to feel your sincerity is there, your trustworthiness is there, your words are believable, and that they have confidence in what you're saying – ONLY THEN will they be willing to purchase.

If you understand that, and you become excellent, you're going to make a ton more money in sales. Think about it. You can make 20 videos (from a well-edited script) in a morning, whereas you couldn't make 20 face-to-face sales calls in a month.

Emerging into this New Normal, your relationship with existing customers is everything. They will be accepting of your offers IF you say the right things.

Think about the opportunity that affords you, and it's now completely acceptable based on what has happened during the COVID period as we were locked down, and even as we were recovering.

Now, if you say, "Jeffrey, my background really sucks." Okay, fix it. Make or create a background or backdrop that you're proud of. Get equipment that makes you look and sound great.

If your living space doesn't look that good, or you don't feel like it's comfortable, then just get an AnyVoo. (UseAnyVoo.com) It brings you an instant great looking office, instant brand, and instant credibility. They give you the whole setup, and they show you how to use it.

You can also shoot on a white wall, shoot by your artwork, shoot by your books, but video is going to be the New Normal in communicating with people.

And Hippo Video (www.hippovideo.io) allows you to make and embed a video into your email without a download. Whoa. Now you can record a video that explains your proposal. Is that cool or what? You can do a follow-up email with a video.

Imagine saying, "Bob, I'm sending you the proposal you requested, but it isn't quite self-explanatory. I want to take one minute to explain how you win when you decide to do business with us." That's what the customer wants to know – how they win. But you can't put that in a proposal. No one's going to read it. BUT THEY WILL WATCH IT.

Before you could attach a video, you sent a proposal by email. The prospect turns to the price. Over. Video is now your new way to say hello. Video is your new way to warm up a customer.

It's video, and it's video *right now.* Take advantage of that opportunity in the New Normal, because I promise you, your competitors may be doing exactly the same thing, and you have to be one notch better in order to be competitive at your price.

NOTE WELL: I have given you my best resources as of this printing. I use all of these resources myself to make and broadcast my virtual/video messages. There are and will be others. Explore and select what's comfortable and most relevant for you, and keep up with what's new.

Video is your new way to convey value. Video is your new way to create a message beyond the proposal. Video is your new way to emotionally communicate with customers in a way that they will find acceptable and, most importantly, buyable.

Jeffrey Gitomer

Ken Walls...
Master of Live Stream...
Shares His
Live Streaming Secrets
and 100 Ideas

The Evolution of Me and Live Streaming

Ustream started doing live streaming events circa 2007, using celebrities as bait. I was seven years late to the game. In 2014, the minute I heard about Live streaming, I started doing it. I immediately saw it as "the future" of personal and corporate marketing.

In the last 2,192 days (that's six years, including two leap year days and six birthdays), there have only been a handful of days that I have NOT gone live. Many days I have been LIVE two, three, or four times in a day.

Along the virtual way, several other companies and platforms started to pop up.

In 2015, live streaming really started to catch on. I was doing live streams on Meerkat and Periscope and delivering valuable content for free... getting myself known. I began picking up thousands of followers on each platform.

Twitter purchased Periscope and integrated it into their platform. Along the way other platforms came along, and some didn't make it. One great platform was Blab, but they just didn't have the funding to continue.

In August of 2015 Facebook began rolling out Facebook Live to high-profile celebrities. By April of 2016, Facebook rolled out Facebook Live to everyone on the platform. Once the 800-pound gorilla threw its hat into the ring, it was game on and game over! With more than 2.6 billion active users per month on the Facebook platform, there has never been a better time to get known, get your brand known, and get your message heard than right now.

Imagine having all of the local television networks (CBS, ABC, NBC, and Fox) call you up and offer to allow you to advertise yourself ANY time you want for AS LONG as you want for free. Would you tell them no? Of course you wouldn't. And yet, there is a MUCH bigger audience on Facebook, YouTube, Periscope, and Twitter that is constantly consuming Livestream content – and most businesses and salespeople are not taking advantage of this FREE audience!

The live streaming arena is constantly changing and improving. Until recently it was very difficult to brand yourself and/or stream to multiple platforms at the same time. Within the last year a new platform, StreamYard, has risen to the top.

StreamYard allows simulcasting to multiple platforms at the same time. So when I go live, I am going live to Facebook, YouTube, Periscope, Twitch, and Twitter, all at the same time. Some are even able to broadcast to LinkedIn Live (based on LinkedIn approval)!

With StreamYard you can add background graphics, intro and outro videos, graphic overlays, lower thirds, multiple guests on at the same time, and so many other cool things. It is a HUGE game changer!

My job in this Gitomer book is to provide you with an understanding and an insight of the untapped value and opportunity to live stream, and the guidance to get you to GO LIVE!

Why Should You Broadcast Live?

Going live is now available on every major social platform – because IT WORKS!

Live streaming lets you create a stronger, more personal relationship with your audience (who could be your customers). ALSO, most platforms give priority algorithms to live video. According to Facebook and others, people (you) spend TRIPLE the amount of time watching live video because it's exciting, in the moment, compelling, and interactive. (OK, cliche: It's the next best thing to being there.)

Live streaming is the #1 way to get eyeballs on you and your content. The Facebook, LinkedIn, Twitter (Periscope), and YouTube algorithms LOVE live streamed content.

Below you will find a handful of live stream secrets along with 100 ideas for live streams!

The simple truth is that people who are not live streaming currently are not doing so because of a handful of reasons.

     a) **They don't feel they have anything of value to talk about.**

     b) **They are afraid of being judged.**

     c) **They feel like too many other people are doing it already.**

     d) **They don't know what to talk about.**

Here is a simple truth about you and YOU doing live stream.

Not everyone is going to like you or what you have to say. That's life. Period. It is unfortunate, but you just cannot get everyone to like you, let alone love you. You HAVE to accept that. Otherwise you will live an entire life, but not "LIVE."

The **BIGGEST QUESTION** to ask yourself is: "What if…?" What if what you have to teach, say, talk about, express, or share with the world could change someone's life for the better?

What if NOT going live and telling your story or sharing your experience, strength, and hope is actually causing someone else to stay in pain? What if you NOT going live and sharing your gift or gifts with the world is stopping your own growth and success?

A lot of people would rather record a video and have it professionally edited than to do a live video. And that's fine to do once in a while. However… you lose the "authenticity factor."

When people are watching a video that was "produced," they subconsciously know that it was, in fact, a produced video. People unconsciously know that you cut out all of the errors.

When you are LIVE… the authenticity factor goes through the roof! People see you as more human (just like they are). They see you as someone that they are just hanging out with.

Below I will list 100 live stream ideas for you to consider as potential ideas for your own live streams.

WHY? People sign onto LiveStream for two primary reasons.

1. **To be entertained.**
2. **To be edu-tained.**

A lot of people would rather record a video and have it professionally edited than to do a live video. And that's fine to do once in a while. However…you lose the "authenticity factor."

Ken Walls

It is human nature to want to hear stories of triumph. We love to hear how someone was on the brink of total annihilation and came back and rose like the Phoenix rising from the ashes!

Get real with yourself so you can get real with people. Be YOU first. Be transparent. Be authentic. Be vulnerable. But above all, Be yourself.

YOU have a story. Tell it. Help people. You have valuable information. Share it. You have messages that others can live better lives from. Deliver them. Staying silent helps no one – especially you.

GROW LIVE Secret #1:

The biggest SECRET to successful live streaming is to NOT give up. I've seen and coached too many people who have started to do live streams and, when they didn't get the audience fast enough, they gave up! They started making excuses for not going live. Too busy, kids stuff, household duties, and a number of other excuses. And so their vision of bringing in new business and customers fizzles, and they start making the descent into what they've "always done."

GROW LIVE Secret #2:

Just be YOU. Be yourself. Don't try to be overly cool and hip… just be you, and be authentic.

GROW LIVE Secret #3:

Deliver VALUE. You can do a live stream showing something you're great at or talk about a chapter in a book you are reading or have read. You can talk about a vacation you took. Talk about writing goals and what it's done for you. There are literally an infinite number of possibilities for the topic of live streams… just make sure you deliver value.

GROW LIVE Secret #4:

Passion. Deliver your message with passion. Period. Nobody likes to share a boring live stream with friends and family. So deliver your message with some enthusiasm and energy!

GROW LIVE Secret #5:

Include your audience. Acknowledge people on your live stream. This is the biggest mistake I see people do. They either do not say hi to people OR, even worse, they spend far too much time saying hi and not delivering a strong message. Say hi quickly… acknowledge folks, and then get to your message. During the delivery of your message you can sprinkle in some more "hi's" and "hello's" as you see new people popping in and out.

Ken Walls

Here are Ken Walls' 100 Grow Live Ideas…

This "starter package of Live Ideas" will get you started.

1. Introduction of YOU! What's your story?
2. How I struggled with _____ and overcame it.
3. What I do to stay organized.
4. How I _____ to bring in new customers (sales and business owners).
5. How my family and I have fun.
6. My favorite hobby is _____. And why I love it!
7. My review of this book _____.
8. The most difficult lesson I've had to learn in business _____.
9. My favorite quote of all time _____.
10. What I do to generate energy when I'm tired _____.
11. How I push through setbacks.
12. Some of the best tips I've learned for marketing my business.
13. My favorite musician or band.
14. Best concert I've ever attended.
15. What I did to face my fear of failure.
16. How I overcame my fear of being judged.
17. How I have burst out of obscurity.
18. Why I have felt like a big failure in the past.
19. The three biggest mantras I live by.
20. Current events in the news.

21. This amazing blessing of today.

22. I am sick and tired of _____.

23. My number one source of inspiration.

24. How I make my product or service irresistible.

25. My mission statement.

26. Top two things I do daily to improve my mindset.

27. My favorite affirmations.

28. When I am feeling down, I _____.

29. Here are a couple of ways I help other people.

30. My favorite recipe is _____.

31. My very first car that I loved was _____.

32. My dream home is _____.

33. If I could have any superpower it would be _____.

34. If I could drive any car it would be _____.

35. My favorite family vacation was _____.

36. How I set my goals.

37. My favorite form of entertainment.

38. What I love most about social media.

39. Why I love holidays.

40. What I do not like about holidays.

41. The things I do to ensure my self-improvement.

42. How to defuse an argument.

43. What is the meaning of life?

44. I want to travel to _____.

45. I want to take my family to _____.

46. How I face imposter syndrome.

47. How my relationship with my _____ has changed my life.

48. When life gets me down I _____ to shift directions.

49. How important is having a positive mindset?

50. How I handle it when people ask me for money.

51. The fastest way out of feeling bad is _____.

52. My #1 goal in life is to _____.

53. If you could relive your _____ what would you do differently?

54. I want to write a book about _____.

55. What's the best thing that happened to you this week? (audience)

56. The funniest thing I've ever seen was _____.

57. My favorite movie of all time is _____.

58. My favorite actor is _____.

59. If my life were to be turned into a movie it would be called _____.

60. I struggled with _____ and overcame it by _____.

61. The most difficult time of my life was _____.

62. How I have successfully built my relationships.

63. The best way to get referrals.

64. I love listening to _____ podcast.

65. The most cost-effective way to promote your business.

66. How I stopped procrastinating.

67. How I use Instagram Stories.

68. One of my favorite things about TikTok.

69. My favorite YouTube channel is _____.

70. Promote your clients/friends.

71. Promote an event for someone else.

72. Promote someone else's book.

73. Teach something that you are passionate about.

74. Teach something that you are an expert at.

75. Talk about common customer problems that you deal with well.

76. Why I pray and/or meditate.

77. Story of adversity that you overcame.

78. How I like to lead.

79. Why are people lost at times and how to get un-lost.

80. What is the true meaning of your life?

81. How to recognize when someone is stealing from you.

82. What social media platforms to use.

83. The content I enjoy seeing most on social media.

84. Livestream (share) your favorite motivational YouTube video.

85. How I set boundaries at work.

86. My top five goals for (year).

87. My favorite way to give back.

88. How I am working to get more YouTube subscribers.

89. I have had it with _____.

90. **How to not be a victim (mindset).**

91. **The #1 way to be a winner.**

92. **How I stopped making excuses.**

93. **Top three books everyone should read immediately.**

94. **Review a movie.**

95. **Q&A: Ask me anything.**

96. **Tips for getting rich.**

97. **When all else fails, do this _____.**

98. **Why my family is the best.**

99. **I am most grateful for _____.**

100. **Why I find gratitude in everything that I do or experience.**

There you go… 100 ideas for live streams. I could literally come up with hundreds more. But I have found that my ideas may not be your flavor – pick 100 for yourself

Two more very important things from Ken Walls:

1. You could do a live stream at 9 a.m. on a subject or topic and then do the EXACT same live stream at 3 p.m. on the same day, and you will quite possibly have two completely different audiences. Even if some of the same people are on the second show, they will NOT remember all of what you talked about.

2. More important than the live streaming *IDEA* is the energy you put into the live stream. People are drawn to live streams with a lot of energy. People love to share live streams that have a lot of energy. Einstein said, "Everything is energy in motion." People are drawn to a live stream because of the energy it is putting out online. I know that may sound a little woo woo foo foo, but I can absolutely promise you that it is true. After more than 2,000 live streams, I can tell you that I have personally experienced it. When my energy has been

low… my viewer count and shares have been low. And the opposite is true as well. If you have a talk with yourself just before hitting that "Go Live" button and hype yourself and your energy up, you will see great results! The most important thing you can do is to put aside the fears of going live, and just Go Live.

I have created a course that teaches all of the elements of live streaming combined with a lot of social media tips and tricks. This course came about as a result of doing more than 2,000 live streams over the past five years. I have coached many people, including some very well-known celebrities, on how to properly live stream.

Each module is packed with multiple video training sessions. Many of these sessions are me sharing my computer screen or my phone screen teaching you exactly how to use apps and technology that is literally at your fingertips!

In the last module (YouTube SEO), I teach you how to INSTANTLY rank a YouTube video to the top of YouTube in minutes (depending on the keyword phrase competition). That module alone is worth thousands of dollars for anyone who wants to build up a presence on YouTube! Go or click here… https://www.growliveacademy.com/a/25532/AUFhkPDF

THANK YOU, KEN WALLS,
for this valuable and actionable wisdom.

CHALLENGE 3 ACTIONS

MASTER VIDEO.

- STUDY Ken Walls documentation of LiveStreaming.
- Make an action plan for platform and content.
- Be certain your virtual background is professional.
- If you need a great background look, go to UseAnyVoo.com.
- Make at least one video a day for 60 days. Save them.
- Practice making videos for free. UseHippoVideo.com.
- Watch your own videos ACTIVELY (take notes to improve).
- Document your successes – small and large.
- Consistency wins.

4
MASTER YOUR
NEW MESSAGING

I'm sitting at my desk, relaxed. I want you to understand that new messaging, especially video and virtual, has to be relaxed in order to be able to be effectively received. Yes, my desk is a little bit messy. I have always said that a clean desk is the sign of a sick mind. It's not my expression; it's somebody else's. But on some people's desks, there's no paper or books or knick-knacks or anything. Seriously? How do they get anything done? How do you smile at "empty"? No, no. I'm giving you the real picture of me.

Now, you may not have my venue. I have a really nice venue. I'm really lucky, but I created my luck by working hard. You can create your own luck. I just gave you the formula: Hard work creates luck!

My secret of success at relaxing is very simple. I surround myself with the things that make me smile. Papers don't make me smile. Therefore I try to have none of them around me. But books make me smile, so I have lots of them. This relaxes me and my message. What makes you smile?

My Steve Jobs business card makes me smile big time, and work to make a dent. And all the things about my grandfather and father's hotel and motel in Atlantic City, New Jersey, make me smile, a plate from Paris, pictures of my friend Dave Winfield make me smile.

All the things that I have in my life that make me smile I have on my desk, and people visiting me will be intrigued and talk about them.

Things that make you smile will also relax you as you're creating your message. Whether you're standing or sitting, have visible things that make you feel good about you. It's not just the engagement of people you're trying to convey a message to. It's the psychological comfort and their safety in deciding to do business with you.

BEWARE: When you're communicating or trying to set a meeting in these new times, you see others trying to set sales appointments and use slide decks, and your boss wants you to make your numbers and have a certain volume of calls.

It's all crap.

The old way is going away. Not going to happen anymore. It's all about your empathy, your understanding, your sincerity, your preparedness, and your message. They will understand you better by listening to your tone and hearing or watching your emotion than they ever could by reading your text. You're asking them how you can help them win, and your performance, your ability to transfer, your message, your social proof, and your customer's perception of you is what will win the day – not some BS "find the pain, challenge the buyer, make insincere offers, manipulate the buyer, or close the sale." OVER.

Now think about that for just a second. All the things that I've just talked to you about have to do with your ability to transfer your message, and convey your message in a way that the other person finds valuable, trustworthy, and acceptable.

The cool news is if you're going to do it from your laptop, rather than face-to-face, you're right at home while you do it. If you connect virtually, you just have to raise your laptop up so that it's at your eye level. You may have to stack it on a bunch of books under your computer, but people can't tell what's underneath. Do it any way you possibly can.

It's more important to make certain that you're conveying your message in a way that is believable… a way that's natural.

It's about being friendly and communicative. It's about having others feel like they're sitting in your kitchen and talking as best friends. You want them to like you. In order to make this happen, you have to like yourself.

I want to feel like you love what you do and you believe in what you do. That's the key. And when you're able to convey that message, you'll know it because every time you make a message, whether it's on QuickTime or Zoom or whatever, you record it and you watch yourself and you listen to yourself and you love it.

Watching yourself is the best coaching you can have. You, looking at you. You, listening to you – that's the real deal. And if you can get yourself to a point where "you like you" (and it's going to take time), your customers will begin responding in a new way. A positive way. A make sales way.

"You watch you" on an everyday basis and I promise you the messaging that you will create and convey will become good, better, and ultimately best. BUT, you have to do it consistently.

I'm 20 plus years into doing it this way. I have a lot of experience. That's why I look and sound relaxed.

I have my own places of comfort. Sometimes I'm sitting in my comfort chair. This is how I convey many of my messages. Other times, like when I'm doing my Facebook live in the morning, which I did every day for months, I'm sitting at my desk or in my library. Sometimes I'm standing because that's the way I want to convey the message.

Look at my videos, both sitting and standing. Get comfortable in both positions by performing in both scenarios. Then determine which suits your message.

IMPORTANT NOTE:
If you're going to message people from your home or from your home office, whether you're sitting or standing, you have to make it look like it's really you. Not formal, just relaxed, real, and friendly.

Your number one job is to figure out what is comfortable for you. Because if you're comfortable, you're going to convey a message of comfort – and vice versa. If you're uncomfortable, you're going to look uncomfortable, sound uncomfortable, and lose the value of positive conveyance.

The customer has to perceive you as being good, being nice, being empathetic, being believable, and your message has to be received by them in an understandable, actionable, and transferable way.

Jeffrey Gitomer

KNOW, THEN MASTER, YOUR VIRTUAL AND VIDEO OPTIONS

What are some of your virtual options? Well, one of the options beyond video or social platforms is a podcast. We have the *Sell or Die* podcast that I do with my wife, the great Jen Gitomer, and we talk about sales, and we interview people, and we talk about what life is like right now in a relaxed and conversational format.

The podcast works because it's real, it's funny, it's relaxed, and it conveys a message of value. Look it up on iTunes and you'll see that we have more than two million downloads. Why? because our podcast is real. Oh, it's rated "E" because every once in a while we'll swear. But you know what the bottom line is? It's us and it's real information that people can use right now, and we interview cool people. You'll love the episodes.

Listen to some of our podcast episodes. Not for our sake – rather to use as a model you can emulate. I want you to listen to them so you'll recognize that podcasting is relaxed, fun, and it could be for you as well.

POWERFUL PODCAST INSIGHT: Invite your customers to be guests on your podcast. Get their CEO to talk about leadership and business philosophy. What do you think is going to happen as a result? Guests will send the episode to everybody. Everyone will see them on a podcast with you. Your audience will grow. Others will request to be guests. It's a solid win for everyone.

NOT SO FAST: You have to be ready to podcast. You have to have the right equipment, broadcast with the right software, use the right recording format, appear on the right platform – for a start. You also have to have great questions to ask guests. Looks like you're going to have to read a book on podcasting.

STUDY KEN WALLS CHAPTER ON WAYS TO GO LIVE. Pick one or two ways that you believe might be of value TO YOUR AUDIENCE.

Why aren't you doing a live broadcast on Facebook? I did one every morning for months. Go to my Facebook page. I have two Facebook pages. I didn't know what I was doing in the beginning, but there's one with kind of a serious picture of me. That's my public page, and every morning at 9:59 a.m. for five months I did a live broadcast, thousands of people were there from all over the world – every day.

It started out with about five people. And it grew, based on the message and word of mouth, to hundreds of people every single morning. By the end of any week, thousands of people have watched and rewatched every episode. SECRET: Then we repurposed the daily live broadcast and posted the daily message on all my other social media platforms.

What do you think that did for me? Many people signed up for my New Normal course because they heard me on my daily Facebook Live, hundreds of people actually. So between Facebook Live and a podcast, you now have a chance to go live and record valuable messages you can turn into money.

NOTE: I got more sophisticated thanks to Ken Walls, and began to broadcast thorough StreamYard.com. It allowed me to go live from Facebook, Instagram. LinkedIn and YouTube at the same time.

You have the opportunity to create a message from wherever you are in the world any time of day or night. Don't waste it.

You can be in a Starbucks, you can be standing on line at the airport waiting to board a plane. You can Go Live from anywhere. But the message that you project has to be understandable, has to be believable, and has to be felt by the recipient as relevant and valuable.

If the listener, your possible sales prospect, feels that way, then your message will be perceived as *transferable*.

MY SECRET: I went live daily for months. Built an audience with valuable content. I connected with customers, connected with people of value, connected with people I knew I could help.

DO THIS: Connect with people who can help you and are compelled to buy into the value of your message, on video. Invite them to join you and participate, and I promise you, you're going to win in the New Normal.

DO THIS: Start a podcast. Study the process. Get inexpensive gear. STUDY Tara Counterman's chapter on Profitable Podcasting. And take the plunge.

My early connecting
philosophy was:
Try to learn
something
about them or
find a common
connection, then
pick up the phone
and call them.
Now I invite them
on our podcast.

Jeffrey Gitomer

Master Profitable Podcasting

By Tara Counterman

Author's Note: Tara Counterman is a successful podcasting entrepreneur. Besides being a wife and mom, that's all she does. Her insights changed our entire podcasting focus and strategy – and it's working. I asked her to create this chapter to help you understand, create, launch, and profit from your podcast.

There is this incredible thing about the internet and digital marketing: They have so much power that they actually give you the ability to collapse time. What else do you know that can do that? And honestly, what other resource is more important than that?

You can *always* create more money.

But time, once it is gone… there is absolutely no bringing it back.

This has never been more evident to me than it has been when watching my children grow. I blink and they have gained six inches and added 500 new words to their vocabulary.

So before I teach you how to utilize podcasts to grow your own big booming business, from the comfort of your own home (yeah, seriously, no fancy studio or equipment required #postpandemiclife), I want you to think about this:

Are you working for your content?

Or is your content working for you?

Tara Counterman

If you are stuck in the hamster wheel of content creation to connect with your audience and sell to them… trust me I get it. I have been there, just like many marketers before you have too. We have this belief that "hard work" breeds success and then wear that like a badge of honor.

Is your content effective? Is there a way you could focus on high-quality content and then repurpose it to serve your audience without doing more work?

Nah, because then you can't wear the busy badge.

Busy has become more important than impact.

The truth though? You can have success without that old, worn and outdated way of thinking. It is 2020 after all, and time to up-level.

Time is the only resource that isn't renewable for you. So let's spend it on high-quality *macro content*. I'll show you how to turn it into money making *micro content* that works for you.

The Profitable Podcast Method was designed to get you off the hamster wheel and owning your own time again. When I was evaluating what we actually did for our clients and the processes that we used I broke it down into five main categories: *Purpose, Plan, Production, Promotion, and Profits*

Each one of these pillars is extremely important to produce a podcast that will not just bring you popularity but will actually produce sales, and impact your bottom line. Before I walk you through them, I want to share with you a visual that will help you understand macro vs. micro content. Having this perspective will allow you to better understand the concepts I am about to share with you.

I see a lot of creators, entrepreneurs, and service providers focusing on the micro content first. When you spend 30 minutes on a written post, well, that post can only be written. Words on a screen don't magically grow a voice or evolve into a video. (Although that would be cool – I don't think even technology is ever going to help on this one.)

And because it will never grow a voice or evolve into a video, it is limited in the ways you can use it. It is beyond imperative that you learn how to leverage macro content in your business. That is why this book was born.

There are so many platforms, and so many ways your customers consume content. The more exposure you have to your ideal client, the more likely they will be to buy from you. Instead of spending 30 minutes… or more… on a written post, what could you do with 30 minutes of video? See the chart on the next page.

CREATING MACRO CONTENT

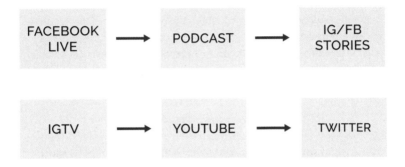

CREATING MACRO CONTENT

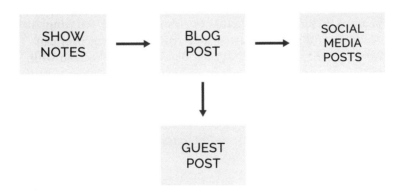

If you instead spend 30 minutes creating high-quality video and audio content, you can leverage your time and energy into hundreds of smaller pieces of content. And if we know anything about social platforms… there are not going to be fewer of them. Platforms will continue to pop up, and your audience will continue to add them to their daily consumption list.

This is why live video is so powerful. You will begin to develop and grow a bank of content that you (or your team) can reach into at any moment and create a whole month of content in a few hours. And you don't even have to be involved.

P-O-W-E-R-F-U-L

So where does a podcast fit into macro and micro content?

Podcasting is one of the most powerful kinds of macro content! Today your ideal clients are busy. Whether they are working a full-time job, multiple jobs, raising kids, trying to now juggle working from home mixed with their kid's distance learning, attempting to stay healthy (maybe even ditching that quarantine 15), or getting sucked into the latest social media trend, they have a lot going on.

You need to meet them where they are and make consuming your content the easiest part of their day. So easy that they can throw on their AirPods, set their phones down, and get on with their lives.

Facebook Lives are great, and for the record, I think should be where you START when it comes to your content workflow. However, they don't offer the same ease of access and availability as a podcast.

A podcast is not only easy to consume for your clients, but they create a space that allows you to build one-way relationships with hundreds, thousands, or even millions of people across the globe. When following the Profitable Podcast Method for your own show you will be able to leverage those relationships right into sales without ever worrying about vanity metrics again.

When podcasting for your business it is extremely important that you are focused on your *purpose*. Everything that you do for your show, from naming, episode topics, formats, and ads, needs to be focused around who your ideal clients are and the journey you are taking them on.

When you know where you want to take them it makes it so much easier to get them there.

Market research is invaluable when it comes to creating content because it allows you to get inside the heads of your ideal clients and uncover the questions they are asking themselves. Even though we have the solution they need, whether that is a product or service, we have to be able to position ourselves as the expert with answers before they make a buying decision.

When you can create the "Woah, they are in my head" effect, you are going to build credibility with your ideal clients quickly. By using the tools available to you through podcasting you can replicate this continuously. Allow yourself to focus on high-quality content that leads your ideal clients to your upcoming offer.

Ideas for market research: Create a survey to send out to your email list, offer a free call, get on sales calls to note all objections and limiting beliefs, do polls or ask open-ended questions on social media.

Where I see podcasters and entrepreneurs fail here is when they stop doing the market research and focusing on their purpose. Everything that goes into your show (and your content in general) should always lead back to serving your ideal clients. Which means getting them closer to investing with you.

This can be done with ONE intentional episode per week, focused on busting limiting beliefs, overcoming objections, and giving them the basics or concepts that your offer or service utilizes.

Always ask yourself: Is spending my time on this focused around my purpose? When you own your own time and have your content working for you, the sales come easier than ever.

Focusing on one intentional episode per week was something that we actually worked on for *Sell or Die*. It is easy to believe that creating more episodes means more downloads, and more downloads means more people listening, and more people listening means more people buying.

BUT that isn't the case.

Your content has to be intentional to turn listeners into buyers. And more isn't always what your ideal client wants or needs. It can actually completely overwhelm them!

That is why it is imperative to know who you are talking to, how they consume content, and meet them where they are. When you focus on one episode per week that has people saying "Woah, you are in my head," you can then spend time driving new traffic to your show. That is how you get more people buying.

ACTION STEPS: Having your content work for you starts by knowing who you are serving. Do some market research and nail down exactly who that is. What are their biggest fears, desires, limiting beliefs, and objections. Once you have completed your research, write out a summary of who your ideal client is. Keep this close and refer back to it often.

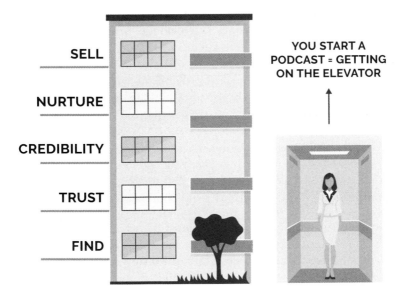

Now that you have your purpose clearly defined we need to focus on a *plan* of action! Utilizing your podcast as a tool to expand your reach means that you need to be efficient and organized in your processes.

Ew, I know I said processes – back end management is the unsexy part of entrepreneurship and sales. I wouldn't bring it up if it wasn't imperative though, so stick with me.

Since you have evaluated where your ideal client is most likely hanging out and consuming content, you know where you should be focusing your efforts. How do you then take one piece of content and turn it into many?

Project Management is going to be key for you. The *Sell or Die* podcast uses Trello to stay organized and on task. Profitable Podcast Productions preferes Asana, and there are dozens of other options out there for you. Just pick one and have a centralized place for all things podcast and repurposing.

You always want to start with the biggest form of content and break it up from there. Your process can look like this:

Go live > Take the audio and edit into a podcast > turn it into an SEO optimized Shownotes post > create 2 podcast social media written posts > create 2 podcast Instagram stories > write an SEO optimized blog post with a second keyword > pin episode to Pinterest > take Shownotes and post as an article on LinkedIn > take blog post and post as an article on LinkedIn > create 3–4 social media posts from the core messages in the recording.

This is just the tip of the iceberg. You can also incorporate YouTube and IGTV. As you can see, there is a lot that can be done to maximize your content, so writing out your plan, creating a digital management system, and staying consistent will always keep you organized.

Of course, planning your systems and structures isn't the only plan you need. You also need to incorporate your podcast into your launch plans! Whether you have a product, service, coaching business, or something else, chances are you are planning big launches or continually launching.

All launching really means is having a set time where you focus on selling something.

When you plan this out for your business, also plan out how you can incorporate your launches. Do you have a course or a few open spots in your agency you want to fill? Plan a launch.

When launching and using your podcast, it is pretty simple. Create a 30–45 second ad that is short and to the point. Keep focused on the transformation your ideal clients want to have or the pain they are trying to avoid.

This ad will change depending on how you are launching and through different phases of your launch, but it is crucial to getting people into your funnel. People do not know you have something to offer unless you make an offer. And when it comes to platforms like iTunes, people don't always realize that the host has a business that could help them even more than consuming their free content.

You. Have. To. Tell. Them.

Make sure that you also always add easily accessible links to the content you are promoting in the description on iTunes and on your podcast website. You want everything to be extremely easy and accessible to your listeners. When people are presented with too many options, or have to search too hard their decision is easy. They stop. They don't buy. So keep it simple and accessible – always!

Most podcasters don't utilize their podcast for their business. They think of it as a separate entity. The place they serve their audience for free, or better yet where they pour countless hours or dollars to just build some brand awareness.

A majority of the experts or gurus in this space are not maximizing what this platform can do for them. Plan it into your launches. Plan to sell on your show.

Then watch what this platform can really do for you.

The next pillar of the Profitable Podcast Method™ is all about *production*. I am going to keep this simple here because, honestly, it is tech heavy and by the time this book is published things could change. Platforms are always evolving. The biggest thing I want to instill in you is that you don't have to do it alone.

If you really want to step into the CEO role of your business. If you want to focus on making sales, and serving your customers then get help on the back end of your podcast. The extent of your involvement when you are able to is planning the content around your launches and other parts of your business and recording the content.

If you are not there yet, don't worry! I remember bootstrapping everything when I started too! There are plenty of free and low-cost tools you can utilize like Audacity for editing and Sonix.ai for transcribing episodes.

And we teach our students to record in the comfort of their own homes with minimal equipment. For high-quality sound grab yourself a microphone (I first started with a $67 one from Amazon), download Zoom, and find a space that has carpet and lower ceilings.

Sound is important when it comes to connecting with your ideal clients. You want to be clear and sound professional, but in no way does that mean you need to pack up and head to a studio to record!

Once you have your episode recorded, it is time to move on to Promotion!

This is where the process gets fun and allows you to work less while building more relationships! I see way too many podcasters spend a lot of time in the back end of their show. Perfecting the way it sounds, loading it into their podcast host, and then only talk about it on social media once.

You are quite literally building a bingeable library of content for your ideal clients to find, binge, and become buyers. When you think about it that way... why wouldn't you *promote* more?

The goal of your episode content is to build relationships, nurture, and prime your listeners for what you offer. When you do that effectively and then drive people to that platform, you are putting them inside of an evergreen funnel that will continuously bring you new clients or customers.

The 80/20 rule is great for keeping yourself in check! Spend 80% of your effort (or your team's effort) on promoting your podcast content and the other 20% of the time creating it.

You never know what is going to speak to the right person at the right time.

Let's say Jeffrey is casually scrolling through social media and comes across a podcast. He has never seen this show before, but the episode topic isn't exactly something that he needs to consume right now. Oh, now he has to run for a meeting. So Jeffrey puts his phone down and doesn't think about it again.

Then a few weeks later the same podcast comes up; this time the topic is something that Jeffrey has been curious about. He reads the post and it definitely sounds like something he needs to listen to. He heads to iTunes, finds the episode, and either listens to it right then or downloads it for the next time he plans to listen to a podcast.

Jeffrey loved the episode, subscribes, continues to listen to new releases, AND went back and listened to previous episodes as well.

Now had the host not promoted their episode or promoted it enough to show up in Jeffrey's feed, they would have missed out on gaining a new avid listener. You never know when the right person is going to be in the right frame of mind to become a superfan.

Do yourself a favor and keep your podcast front of mind for your followers.

And finally, the moment I know you have been most waiting for. Tara, how do I use my podcast to generate **PROFIT**?

By following all of the recommendations in this chapter, and book, you are already well on your way! But let me leave you with a few more tips to create a podcast that brings your business more profits.

1. **Always focus on your ideal client and the transformation they are on.** What do they need to see, hear, feel, and know in order to believe that you are the expert who can take them to where they want to go.

2. **Plan your podcast into your launches.** Incorporate your own ad strategy (not third party sponsored ads). If you are doing a live series on Facebook or another platform, take the audio, put it on your podcast, and be sure to clearly link where your listener can sign up. Bring on past clients as guests and discuss their transformations with your program or service.

3. **Utilize affiliate marketing.** Whether asking guests of your show if they have an affiliate program for what they want to promote (or making it a requirement) or adding in links to your Shownotes and descriptions for things that you are an affiliate for, affiliate marketing can be an added revenue stream for you!

4. **Think outside of the box.** Always look for ways to innovate and incorporate what works on your other platforms into your show.

Podcasting can be a huge piece of your marketing and revenue driving strategy.

It will require you to think outside of the box…
To look past the industry norms…
And to incorporate it into your business.

When you are able to master those things, it is the platform that will keep on giving. So what are you waiting for?

Head over to profitablepodcastproductions.com/golive for more free resources to help you profitably podcast. See you there!

CHALLENGE 4
ACTIONS

MASTER YOUR NEW MESSAGING.

- Create a space for yourself that looks great to your audience.
- Discover and implement your best virtual background options.
- GO LIVE on Facebook or one of the major social media platforms and talk about your expertise once a week.
- Watch your own videos ACTIVELY (take notes to improve).
- Make and implement a content repurposing plan.
- STUDY Tara Counterman's piece on Profifable Podcasting.
- Follow Tara's podcast action plan.
- Start a podcast with a subject that would attract customers and prospects.
- Watch your own podcast ACTIVELY (take notes to improve).
- Invite c-level customers as your first friends.
- Make and implement a content repurposing plan.
- Consistency wins.

5
MASTER YOUR SOCIAL MEDIA

What is your present social footprint? (Who are you in front of?)

How many social connections do you have? (Who are you connected to?)

What are you doing to stay top of mind? (What value messages are you posting?)

How many social connections do you WISH you had? (Way more than you have?)

If I google you personally, what shows up? (Do you dominate the first few pages?)

That's what your prospect or your customer sees. (OUCH!)

STRATEGY: Where do your customers go? Go there!

How do your customers find you now? Be there more often with a value message!

Where do you wish they went to find you? Invite them!

My challenge to you is very simple: Build your social value presence, and double your social connections.

Personally, I wanted to expand my social footprint, so I went live on Facebook every day for months. It worked. Thousands and thousands of people from all over the world attended my daily event, and as a result, more people followed me.

You should go live once a week. You need to visit all of your platforms where you post and interact and engage daily with the people who interact and engage with you, especially on LinkedIn, because that's the business platform.

On LinkedIn, you can create appointments from connections, you can start to message people its your first connection with, or you want to be connected with, but there has to be something of value. A download, an ebook, something people would consider valuable, something they might share with others, and then you can begin appearing on other live and pre-recorded broadcasts to boost your reach.

My social footprint has been exponentially increased and improved by doing a podcast that attracts people to my social footprint. All of these opportunities are available right now – almost all of them are free. You have an amazing opportunity and an ability to present an attractive, value-based message that builds your stature and reputation.

That's the real opportunity.

Make a goal, and have an *intention* to be more present and *interactive* on social media. Do it on every single platform. Where do you start? It's easier to start on LinkedIn. Where do you go after that? It's still pretty easy. You go to Facebook, but where do you go after that? Well, that's going to depend on where your customers go. You might want to go to YouTube or Instagram and search.

If you're B2B, you may want to double down on LinkedIn and go live or go live on Facebook, but whatever you decide to do, have a YouTube channel with your testimonials on there as well.

Your social footprint, your social presence, is your message power and your brand power, both corporately and personally. And you can create it with a time investment. In the same amount of time you're wasting binge-watching some Netflix show, you could be posting value-based messages and mastering your social outreach and social footprint. My challenge to you is that it's no longer an option.

"Well, Jeffrey, I don't do Twitter." Well, 500 million people do do Twitter. You might want to give it a shot. And by the way, this is not just a challenge, this is calling you out on your wasted opportunity, your lost opportunity to brand yourself and your reputation.

NOTE WELL: Wherever your customers are, wherever your customers go socially, that's where you need to be front and center with a message of value, not a sales pitch.

The NEW TRUTH about closing the VIRTUAL SALE.

Every salesperson is looking for the fastest way, the best way, and the easiest way to "close" a sale.

More than human nature, for salespeople, closing the sale is both a desire and a need. And the results are totally measurable. Either you win, or you lose. There is no second place in sales.

Many people think that "closing the sale" is the fulcrum point of the process. All of those people are wrong, especially in the virtual world. Closing the sale begins BEFORE the sales presentation begins.

The customer is googling you DURING your virtual presentation. They want proof so that they're confident to move forward.

Jeffrey Gitomer

A sale is not "closed." A sale is *earned*. And "social proof" is the BEST way.

In my career I have learned two powerful words that complete the selling process. They allow me to complete the sale without a feeling of discomfort or hesitancy. When it's time to deliver those words, I know in my heart of hearts the sale is mine.

The two words are: FAIR ENOUGH, and they are delivered to the prospect in the form of a question. "Fair enough?"

"Fair enough" are the most powerful words to affirm the prospect's intention to buy. You may be erroneously referring to the prospect saying "yes" as "closing a sale." Not good.

"Fair enough" asks for a commitment and validates the value and the fairness of your offer. If your offer is valuable, or perceived as valuable by the prospect, then the words "fair enough" will always be followed by the prospect's affirmative answer. And vice versa.

The words "Fair enough" are also a self-test. Do you perceive that your offer is so valuable that when you ask the prospect, "Is that fair enough?" you know in your mind and in your heart that in fact it IS fair enough. Always ask yourself the "fair enough" question BEFORE you give a sales presentation. If you can answer "yes" to your own offer, it's likely the prospect will answer "yes" as well.

Does your online social proof affirm your "fair enough" question?

The words "fair enough" ask for a "yes" and a confirmation to move forward. They are direct, completely understandable, and are non-manipulative. They don't contain the phrases, "Can you see any reason not to move forward?" or worse, "Is there any reason you could not do this today?" Those are old-world, BS sales expressions of the worst order.

"Fair enough" is pointed, powerful, and positive. And you don't have to wait until the end of your presentation to ask. You can slip it in once or twice as you're presenting to make certain you and the prospect are in agreement and moving forward.

"Fair enough" gives you a transition from your presentation to earning the business.

THINK ABOUT THIS: If you have a bunch of presentation slides and offer to send some kind of proposal at the end of your presentation, you can never use the words "fair enough."

Your job as a salesperson is to figure out how your presentation can culminate with the words "fair enough" and that there's enough perceived value and social proof in your presentation for the customer to say, "Yes, that's fair enough."

If the prospect says, "That sounds fair enough," or gives you some form of yes, that's not just a purchase, it's also a report card that your offer was perceived as valuable enough to move forward.

START HERE: Before you do virtual presentations, review your entire sales presentation and see where the words "fair enough" fit into it. If there's no place for them, then your offer is most likely not fair enough, and will be met with some kind of resistance or stall.

This review process requires work on your part, and may mean you have to build your online presence and earn more social proof.

Once your online presence is solid and has been established, revise your sales presentation. This is a good thing! It will most likely mean you have to ask more questions, discover what the buying motive of the prospect is, and make certain you have value offerings that are in harmony with their true needs and motives to buy.

If you are able to give prospects the answers they're hoping for, you will have created the ultimate buying experience. Asking the question "fair enough" will become a joy. A financially rewarding joy.

I just provided you with a major secret of selling – a secret that, when mastered, has the potential to double your sales and increase your earnings significantly. All you have to do is create a strategy to incorporate it.

Fair enough?

CHALLENGE 5
ACTIONS

MASTER YOUR SOCIAL MEDIA.

Social media platforms are your (free) way to reach the world in a nanosecond. The challenge is to connect with YOUR world, and influence and attract them with your message. The key word of understanding how to make attraction and influence happen is "VALUE."

- Register and start/create/improve a page on every platform.

- Concentrate on the platforms your customers and prospects visit the most, but don't ignore platforms where YOU can be informed and influenced.

- During your morning routine, write a few value-messages you can post.

- Don't be afraid to ASK for response and opinion.

- If you're going to make offers (sell something) make it value-first. A list, a graphic, an article – something of value. Something of interest. Grab their email from their response and sell from there. VALUE FIRST.

- If no one responds or buys, DON'T QUIT – FIX IT.

- Collect and earn SOCIAL PROOF. If your customers love you, love your product or service, and love the work you do, ask them to say so socially.

Master your social footprint by doubling your social outreach and your QUALITY social connections.

Jeffrey Gitomer

6
MASTER YOUR
SOCIAL MEDIA PROOF

Are you a 5?

Think about how you rate and give feedback. Do you give 5 stars for a book or a restaurant or a hotel or a bar or a beer? Fewer than 5 stars? Have you ever rated a product that you bought on Amazon? Of course you have. Sometimes you have even left a comment.

After people purchase products or visit places, they rate their purchase or their experience from 1 to 5. TripAdvisor, Yelp, Amazon, cars, Airbnb. Even employers. It's a global phenomenon, and it's here to stay.

So let's reverse the question: **Are you a 5? Ouch!**
Would your customers rate you a 5?
Would your social connections rate you a 5?
Would your boss or your employer rate you a 5?

"Five stars" is social proof. So, how do you prove your "5" if there is no rating? There are other ways to get a 5. You can get referrals from people, you can get written comments or videos from the voice of your customers posted on social media.

Do you earn 5's or ask for them? It's far better if you earn them. Unsolicited praise. That is the secret. You should receive them for a reason. Maybe you gave amazing service, maybe your quality is amazing, maybe you did something memorable, or maybe it was just easy to do business with you. Whatever it is or was, that praise is better than thousands of ads bragging about yourself.

The power of a 5… let me share with you what the power of that is. The voice of your customer is a thousand times more powerful, maybe a million times more powerful than yours. It's proof. The final frontier of consumer believability.

Jeffrey Gitomer

Unsolicited praise earns unsolicited referrals.

Jeffrey Gitomer

When you say it about yourself, it's bragging. When customers say it about you, it's proof. You're wanting your customers to say something great about you in text or, more powerfully, say something in a video – a video about a remarkable service that you provided or about some event that took place, or about something that you said, or some action that took place.

They're bragging about you or your business in a way you never could. That social proof will lead you to way more business than you could ever solicit for yourself.

And so a big key for you in this New Normal is to build remarkable service-based relationships with your customers to a point at which they're happy and willing to say something about you in video on social media.

Because if they're not, you're going to have to be bragging about yourself all the time. And that's not going to work in the New Normal. What will work in the New Normal is people coming online in droves to talk about how great you are.

PROOF of PROOF: As you have read, I did a Facebook Live for an extended period of time, I did it every morning at 9:59 a.m. I have about 500 testimonials thanking me for what I've done. It's a blessing.

I can put those words of praise anywhere. I can post them anywhere. If I asked for videos on my Facebook page, I'd get 100 of them tomorrow. In fact, I think I will. But the bottom line for you; you have to earn it. You cannot just ask for it.

You must earn that right. And then customers will gladly say, okay. This is your time to emerge – socially.

Everyone is finally accepting it. People who were home for a month or two were online and virtual every day. People meeting on Zoom, Facebook, LinkedIn, Microsoft Meetings, even Skype. Virtual meetings and sales calls of all kinds are now "normal." Live meetings and social participation are now "normal."

Your job is to build your social platform to a point where it's so valuable that people are willing to speak up on your behalf and thank you for what you're doing, and tell other people how great you are. They're sharing your excellence. Is that cool or what?

CHALLENGE 6
ACTIONS

MASTER YOUR SOCIAL MEDIA PROOF

- What actions are you taking on behalf of your customers that they would go on your social platforms and rate you a 5 or give you a video testimonial?

- It's OK to ask for a social comment. ONCE.

- All your customers are going to look for proof that you are who you say you are and that your product or service is what you say it is – JUST LIKE YOU DO.

- Ask for or earn social proof or testimonials for every one of your social platforms. NOT AN OPTION.

- The more proof you post, the more Mother Google will love you.

REALITY:
Social proof will bring you business, but you can't ask for it or get it unsolicited if you have not earned it.

Jeffrey Gitomer

7
MASTER HUMOR

Why is humor so important in the New Normal?
Because people need to laugh.

That's why Chapter Eight in *The Little Red Book of Selling*, which you own, or should own, is titled: "If You Can Make Them Laugh, You Can Make Them Buy."

I don't recommend telling jokes. It's not "three guys walking into a bar." It's telling stories that other people can relate to, that they find humorous, and are emotionally engaging. They don't have to laugh out loud, but they do have to smile.

Stories trump jokes.

MAJOR CLUE: Humor is the highest form of intelligence. If you learn a foreign language, humor is the hardest part to learn. Humor relaxes. It sets a mood. Humor creates tacit approval when the other person laughs. It relaxes the other person when you tell a story about something that happened that makes them smile or laugh. And I think that's the most important part of humor's power. People relate to you through laughter.

Here's a smile. I hope it relates to you. During the COVID pandemic we were locked in and had to clean our own space. Yes, we had a housekeeper, but now it's all on us. Our daughter, little 11-year-old Gabrielle Gitomer, was part of the cleaning crew. I said, "Gabrielle, go grab that mini shop-vac thing and clean up this chair." "Okay, fine, daddy," she says, and grabs it out of the holder. A first-time user, she doesn't quite know how to start it. She clicks a button and it opens up and releases all the dirt from the vacuum onto the floor. We were howling and it gave us something to laugh in concert about. Spontaneously laughing together about something funny not only relaxes people, it actually makes people pay attention. You tell stories that tie in or lead to your message.

I've been studying humor for more than 50 years. My library is full of Groucho Marx, *The Honeymooners*, with Jackie Gleason, Audrey Meadows, Art Carney, and Joyce Randolph is my favorite sitcom of all time. I have several signed books and photos of all of them. I surround myself with things that I love and things that make me smile. You can see smile things when you visit my surroundings.

A poster of Lucy (from the "Peanuts" cartoon) saying, "Vote for the blockhead of your choice," and Fonzie, and Alfred E. Neuman, and the things that I have grown up with that have made me smile and made me laugh.

Humor is relaxing to me, not just to the other person, and it makes me feel good on the inside. I read humor passages all the time, whether it's cartoons or funny stories or books, or I look at humor art… all things that keep me in a great frame of mind.

NOTE WELL: It's not just what you do to convey your message. It's how you build your own internal attitude… with smiles, humor, and laughter.

STOP THIS, START THAT: Stop watching violence and start watching funny. Any kid's movie has amazing humor in it. Watch those.

You can best transfer your message with humor. It makes the other person feel closer to you because you've made them laugh. If you can make people laugh, you can make them buy.

And keep in mind that at the end of humor is the hype of listening. You go to a comedy club. You sit there and listen to the comedian; he makes you laugh and your drink is coming out of your nose. And then he starts to talk again. Everyone is quiet cause you don't want to miss what's next. At the end of humor is the attention to listening.

**Study humor to a point
until you become
familiar enough
with it to use it.**

**Tell a story that makes
the other person smile
and you will relax
them enough to like
you, relate to you,
engage with you,
and ultimately,
buy from you.**

Jeffrey Gitomer

Having the first laugh makes a sale that lasts.

Hey, I got a new photo. It's about time – the other one was four years old. I've lost a bit of hair since the last one – OK, OK, I've lost a lot of hair since the last one. But I couldn't tell – they fell out one at a time.

There are two ways of looking at my hair loss.

1. **Oh, my gosh, I'm losing my hair – woe is me.**
2. **There's not much more to lose.**

I have tried to use my misfortune (if you want to look at the vain side) as an opportunity to poke fun at myself and make others laugh.

For example, in a seminar I'll say "I'm not actually losing my hair – I'm a hair donor. I give my hair to people less fortunate than myself" – and I'll point to someone with lots of hair. And I'll add, "The Hair Club for Men refused to let me join. They said you have to have *some* to get in."

Or I'll say, "I wear great ties, because I know no one is ever going to come up to me and say 'Jeffrey – Great hair!'"

The hair thing has been beneficial financially – for example, I use very little shampoo – and even less conditioner. It takes me very little time to comb my hair – giving me lots of time to work on other beauty areas.

Last week someone wanted me to describe myself so I could be met at the plane. I said, "I'm six feet tall, weigh about 185, have a beard, my hair is short – and some of it's missing" (my customer howls with laughter).

The other day in Dallas I needed a haircut and was in one of those snazzy hotels. I figured "How expensive can it be?" and went ahead without asking the price. Fifty bucks they charged. I asked the guy – "What is it – a dollar a hair?"

Well, the humor thing seems destined to be in my presentation material, because the hair thing definitely is not. What's your humor point? Do you have one?

The Major Clue: Making people smile or laugh puts them at ease and creates an atmosphere more conducive for agreement. If they agree with your humor, they are more likely to agree with purchasing your product or service.

- *Pick something that's funny to you.* The lack of hair used to bug me – now it doesn't (as much). Now I look for ways to laugh about it – because I can't change it.

- *Pick something that's personal to you.* If it's about you, it's comfortable to you.

- *Develop lines that are tested to make people laugh – nothing corny.* Try out the lines on your friends and co-workers first. If they laugh – use them. If they groan, so will everyone.

- *Keep the lines clean.* Real clean.

- *Be careful about ethnic or gender humor.* My recommendation is – don't.

- *Poke fun at yourself.* It's OK if the finger points at you. It's NOT OK if you make fun at the expense of others.

- *Don't drag it out.* Use it once or twice and move on.

- *Take small humor risks.* If the other guy is bald, I say, "You know, the first thing I liked about you was your hair." He laughs and we grow a bit closer having a "plight-in-common."

I believe that making people smile is a major key in selling. Prospects may not be interested in hearing about your stuff, but they're always looking to smile or laugh.

Want some safe topics?

- **children (what they did or said)**
- **traffic (what you did or saw)**
- **repeating a sitcom or television line (with acknowledgments to the source)**
- **self-stuff (hair, clothes, make-up, shoes)**
- **self-abilities (golf, tennis, running, exercise)**
- **self-improvement (frustrations climbing the ladder or studying)**

Developing humor takes time. Like all other sales skills, it must be learned. And yes, some people are "naturally funnier" than others. BUT if you're not very funny, you can learn. The best way I've found is to pay attention to what happens to you.

The other day I was in the shower in a hotel and broke open a new bottle of shampoo. After I used it and put the lid back on, I remarked to myself, "You know you don't have much hair when you use the shampoo and you can't tell any is missing." I laughed at myself. Do you?

"If you can make 'em laugh, you can make 'em buy"

Jeffrey Gitomer

A lesson from a laugh.
Listen to this one.

Ho, ho, ho.

No, it's not Christmas. But it is the season to be jolly. Jolly is always in season. Some people look at it as a "laugh." I look at it as a learning device, listening tool, attention grabber, self-healer, powerful selling tool, and – of course – fun.

An airline flight attendant from Alaska Airlines started his "flight safety announcements" with the statement: "Welcome to Alaska's flight #320 to San Francisco – if you're not headed to San Francisco, now would be a great time to get off the plane, and one of our friendly gate agents will steer you in the right direction."

I was smiling – so were the rest of the passengers.
I was listening – so were the rest of the passengers.

My name is Mark, I'm the lead flight attendant." He continued, "My ex-wife Sandra, and her new boyfriend, Bill – will be serving you in the back cabin today. This should make for an interesting flight." Now I was laughing (and listening). And so was every passenger on the plane. And I listened to EVERY WORD he said from then on.

Some years I get into airplanes more than 100 times, and I NEVER listen to the safety instructions – oh, I hear them mumbling, but I don't LISTEN (pay attention) to them. This one flight was different. After the first joke, I was listening for the next joke (and to the instructions) – this guy was genuinely funny.

The object of the safety instructions, or any oral communication, is to get people to LISTEN. Otherwise, why make it? If you've ever seen the way "safety instructions" are given on an airplane, you'd howl. One attendant hides behind a wall and reads a script in a monotone, while another robotically goes through the motions of pantomiming what the other has said. It's a joke – but a pathetic one. No one listens.

On the newer planes, they now have safety videos where one person of every race, creed, and religious orientation is in each scene, and all of them are plastic (with a white male pilot, of course). This technological innovation does have one thing in common with its "human" predecessor – no one pays attention. It's dull. Their communication is without an iota of a compelling reason to listen. In the beginning they beg you to pay attention to this IMPORTANT safety announcement. No one does – not even the flight crew.

Are people listening to you? Are you sure?

Are they listening to your presentation? Are you sure?

Are they paying attention to your important communications? Are you sure?

MAJOR CLUE: How much humor is in your communication?

Here's the rule: Laughter leads to listening.

Whatever you say AFTER you say something funny will be heard and remembered 10 times more than to drone on and "think" or "expect" that others hear them – much less are listening. *In short, laughter leads to listening and creates the highest listening environment.*

What makes laughter make people listen better? Easy – people would rather be laughing. After the first laugh you want – maybe even expect – another. I wasn't disappointed with that Alaska flight attendant. After the first round of laughs, he continued: "If you're caught smoking, we throw you off the plane immediately. And for those of you who brought a TV with you on board, it will not work." Then he gave the announcement about smoking and electronic devices. Perfect. Laugh, then listen. Every person on the plane was paying complete attention.

What can the power of laughter do for you and your sales? Listen up. (Please pay attention, this is REALLY, REALLY important.) After laughter:

- **The prospect is listening.**
- **The prospect is more "in the mood" to buy.**
- **During your talk, the prospect is on the edge of their seat listening for what's next.**
- **During your one-hour sales presentation, the prospects won't look at their watch ONCE.**
- **"Funny" bridges the gap between professional and friendly.**

Got humor? To get a laugh, here are a few things you'll need to do:

1. **Test your humor on a friend to be sure it's funny before you say it.**
2. **Make sure the laugh is at your own expense, not at someone's else's.**
3. **Not funny? Study humor.**
3.5 **Timing is everything – study comedians – they know HOW and WHEN to deliver a punch line, and how long to pause.**

And beyond the listening and the understanding by the prospect, the most powerful, unspoken part of laughter is that it's *tacit approval.*

A prospect's laughing is a form of personal agreement.
Once you get tacit approval (i.e., they like you), then all you need is verbal approval, and you have the order. Then the joke's on the competition.
Ho, ho, ho.

Jeffrey Gitomer

May the joke be with you...

Need to improve your humor?
Become a student of humor.

1. **Visit comedy clubs.** Study delivery and timing. Watch audience reaction. Observe what makes them laugh. What makes you laugh?

2. **Watch comedy shows on TV/cable.** The older shows tend to be funnier. Make a note of what's funny. Bugs Bunny is funny. Actions, vocal tones, facial expressions, words, types of stories.

3. **Read joke books or books that are funny.** Milton Berle's joke book is particularly good. Books written by humorists like Dave Barry, Art Buchwald, and Lewis Grizzard are great.

4. **Join Toastmasters.** They have advanced programs in humorous speaking.

5. **Watch and listen to children very carefully.** Kids are naturally funny in both words and actions.

6. **Read history.** The truth is often stranger and funnier than fiction.

7. **Take humor risks where you don't have much to lose – at home, with friends, in divorce court, in prison, etc.**

8. **Take a professional comedian or joke writer to lunch.** By spending time with professionals you will learn the make-up of humor.

9. **Practice making funny faces and gestures in the mirror.** If you're really brave, use the rear view mirror.

10. **Get out your high school yearbook.** Talk about funny – look up your picture. Or your girlfriend's.

11. **Take an acting class.** This is a good way to come out of your shell. A friend of mine told me that I was acting like a jerk. I told him I wasn't acting.

12. **Carry audio tapes of your favorite comedians with you in the car.** Pop them in before you make a sales call to get a lift (or an idea).

13. **Start looking for humor in your everyday life.** Try to appreciate it as it is happening, instead of always in hindsight.

14. **Practice exaggerating your gestures and experimenting with your posture.** A lot of humor is body language humor. Learn to be funny without saying a word.

15. **Hang around funny people.** It's amazing how your humor will increase when you're in the company of people who are funny.

15.5 **Laugh a lot.** If you're serious about using humor, start smiling and laughing more.

CHALLENGE 7 ACTIONS

MASTER HUMOR.

- Read and study chapter eight in *The Little Red Book of Selling*, which you own, or should own, titled: "If You Can Make Them Laugh, You Can Make Them Buy."

- Humor is a way of life, not a subject.

- My philosophy has always been: Lead with humor.

- Study humor of every sort. Not just to laugh, but WHY it makes you laugh.

- Document everything funny that's happened to you and see how it can fit into your presentation.

- Tell stories, not jokes.

- This chapter is filled with gold. STUDY IT.

8
MASTER CREATIVITY

My whole life I've been able to come up with ideas, and I have always wondered why the hell, how the hell am I able to come up with them? Maybe it's because I read books on creativity. But, maybe more.

Here are things I do besides my morning routine. Individually they are not the root of my creative process, BUT collectively they are the elements that allow my ideas to surface or appear…

- **Stay sober**
- **Text myself**
- **Limit phone and computer distractions**
- **Limit notifications to text messages**
- **Limit TV distractions**
- **Write down EVERYTHING before I go to bed**
- **Have conversations with smart people**
- **Read every day**
- **Write every day**
- **Use humor to communicate**
- **Give talks**
- **Maintain a YES Attitude**

THINK: Why is creativity important to you? What can it do for you?

I'm going to try to explain it in the easiest way possible. When I read the book *Thinkertoys* by Michael Michalko, I got my creative AHA! I learned that I could actually create ideas based on the way I looked at things, and based on the way I perceived things.

There's a creativity model in the book called SCAMPER. It's an acronym all about the questions you ask yourself (or a group) to come up with creative alternatives to common ideas, or common things, or old ways of looking at or doing things.

Things like your logo, business card, mission statements, sales presentations, or product offerings. How do you look at your old or tired things? SCAMPER asks: What can you *substitute*? What can you *combine*? What can you *adapt*? What can you *modify*? What can you *magnify*? What can you *minimize*? What can you *put to other uses*? What can you *eliminate*? What can you *rearrange*? Those are the questions that make you think about how to come up with a new idea.

Thinkertoys by Michael Mihalko is the best book on creativity ever written. Give it to yourself. Study it. His second book, *Cracking Creativity* is equally as powerful. If you want more advanced elements of creativity, go buy Edward de Bono's books on lateral thinking and serious creativity.

It's a science. You can learn it. So here is the final book on creativity that I want to share with you. It's called *What a Great Idea*. You see, ideas rule when you're going to see a customer or when you're trying to build a relationship with a customer.

Let's take a business card I saw as an example of amazing creativity. This card is a bag from a store in Venice, Italy. The store is called Empressa. They had the coolest clothing I've ever seen – and bought. As I was checking out, and the guy was putting my purchases in their beautiful red bag, I said, "Can I have your business card? I'd like to buy things from you when I get back to America." He says, "Sure." And he gives me a tiny replica bag. Come on! And then he puts the receipt inside the business card bag.

This is by far one of the most creative uses of a business card ever.

"Set yourself an idea quota for a challenge you are working on, such as five new ideas every day for a week. You'll find the first five are the hardest, but these will quickly trigger other ideas. The more ideas you come up with, the greater your chances of coming up with a winner."

Michael Michalko,
Thinkertoys: A Handbook of Creative-Thinking Techniques

The overlooked power that may be your sales Kryptonite.

I see, therefore I learn.
I see, therefore I think.
I learn and I think, therefore I reason and respond.

THE POWER: That is the power of observation.

How are you taking advantage of that power?
How would you rate your power of observation?

What are you looking at, and how does what you see impact your world, your education, your sales, your career, your success, your family, and your life?

HISTORICAL OBSERVATION: In 1939, when Napoleon Hill completed the best sales book ever written, *How to Sell Your Way Through Life,* he included "The habit of observation" as one of the 28 qualities all master salespeople must possess. Here are his exact words: *Habit of observation. The super-salesman is a close observer of small details. Every word uttered by the prospective buyer, every change of facial expression, every movement is observed and its significance weighted accurately. The super-salesman not only observes and analyzes accurately all that his prospective buyer does and says, but he also makes deductions from that which he does not do or say. Nothing escapes the super-salesman's attention!*

HISTORICAL OBSERVATION: Ten years ago, people looked around and used what they saw to both learn and reason. To think and create experiences. To learn lessons and grow. Life lessons.

PRESENT OBSERVATION: Today everyone has a smartphone and a tablet. And the power of observation is fading into the lure of the electronic siren.

Yes, I look at my iPhone too, but I'm consciously trying my best to limit/reduce my "stare time." I'm only "notified" (interrupted) when my phone rings or if I get a text.

Yes, I use apps as necessary to wake me or help me find my way. And I use my phone as a camera, documenting what I observe, and occasionally posting my observations on Instagram (@jeffreygitomer if you're interested in what I see). I receive no social media notifications, no email notifications, and none of the other dings, bells, and whistles that are offered on the electronic siren.

REASON: Interruption of thought is where focus is lost.
REASON: Interruption of thought is where ideas get lost.

When you look at something, observe something, it triggers a powerful mental response, IF you are focused.

- **An idea**
- **A past experience**
- **A fact you want to convey**
- **You're developing a strategy.**
- **You're capturing a thought (voice to text, please).**
- **It enables you to deepen the conversation.**
- **It helps you make a point.**
- **It solidifies your thinking.**
- **You can uncover a motive.**
- **You can find common ground.**
- **You can build rapport.**
- **You may even get an AHA! from unfinished thoughts or projects.**

Observation is both seeing what's around you, and thinking what's about you. When you're thinking and staring off into space, you may not be looking at anything in particular, but your *mental* observation is being called into play.

REALITY OBSERVATION: I see people get off the plane and walk into a wall while reading or texting, and think nothing of it.

Smartphone or no smartphone, most people are not observant, let alone paying attention to their surroundings. The smartphone has merely increased that lack of observation, not created it.

Whatever the outcome is from your observations, they have added to your wealth. Wealth or knowledge, experience, and insight.

The reality is I'm writing this article that will get millions of views, be made into a YouTube video, appear in my weekly email magazine, become a power lesson on GitomerLearningAcademy. com, and later appear in one of my books, while most people are staring at their phones. And while I realize that that's a general observation, there is no doubt that the world has become much less observant in the last five years. Especially the sales world. Maybe even you.

The reason I'm writing this is that I just returned from eight days in Paris – arguably the most beautiful city in the world, and most people there were not looking. Dude, look at your phone later, YOU'RE IN PARIS!

No matter what I recommend, each of you reading this will justify your own situation and circumstance: whether it's speed of response, need to communicate with customers, need for immediate information, or the simple desire to be "in the know" and "in the now." With your head buried in your phone. Not paying attention to the world around you with the things around you. Cheating yourself out of your competitive advantage. And keep in mind, that's just my opinion.

- **Access your phone when you're at home or in the office alone.**

- **Access information when you want to, not when you hear a beep.**

- **Turn off social media notifications during the day.**

NOTE WELL: Yes, speed of response is important, but if you must ding, use it as a *choice* rather than a *must*.

MENTOR LESSON: "Antennas up!" My mentor and friend, the late great Earl Pertnoy, said. He smiled as he spoke. It was one of his early pieces of advice to me. "Pay attention to every detail around you. People and things," he said. I always did. That was 35 years ago. I still do.

That simple, but powerful piece of advice has helped me earn a fortune. And it can do the same for you.

How are you using the power of first impression?

You have THE meeting. The CEO has agreed to give you 30 minutes. This is the opportunity you have been hoping – working – for.

Now is the time to hone your presentation to perfection… or is it?

Do you honestly think the CEO wants to hear you rant for 30 minutes about you, your company, and your product?

First of all, he or she will most likely decide in five minutes or less if you are someone they want to do business with. And second of all, whatever you're selling, chances are he or she already knows about it.

Now is the time to prepare a greeting, an opening exchange, and 10 killer questions that separate you from the competition.

And you better figure out what the brief opening exchange will consist of.

You gonna give the CEO your crappy business card? Or worse, your literature?

You probably believe you have the best product or service in the market – now tell me your business card is the BEST you have ever seen. And that your literature is the same: BEST.

Yeah, right. Your literature is self-serving, and your business card is somewhere between a joke and embarrassing. Certainly not BEST.

HISTORY: I have asked 500 audiences the question, "Which do you think is a more powerful way for me to make a first impression, with my business card or with an autographed copy of one of my books?" They unanimously answer, "With your book." (And keep in mind I have a GREAT business card.)

Then I ask, "Which do you think is a more powerful way for me to make a business first impression, with my brochure or an autographed copy of one of my books?" They unanimously answer "With your book."

And the same audience goes out the next day and they introduce themselves with a business card and a brochure.

I don't get it.

I have given them the answer to a powerful business introduction, and they don't change a thing.

In their minds they think, "I don't have a book," or "I haven't written a book," or "What would I write a book about?" Or they think, "This is what my company gave me, and I'll just wait until they give me something else," and drop the thought, even though it would make an incredible impact on their first impression and their credibility. In short, they are giving up their edge, their WOW.

I don't get it.

Salespeople are looking to differentiate themselves. They are looking to provide some value beyond their product or service to the customer. They are looking for something that will prove to the customer that they are superior to their competition. They moan that their product (whatever it is or isn't) is becoming a commodity. And they don't do anything about it.

I don't get it.
Do you get it?
What are you willing to do?

What are you willing to change, so that when you do get that CEO meeting you are ready to make a great first impression, an impressive first impression, a differentiating first impression, and earn a sale?

Here are a few things you can do that will help:

- **Change your title.** Make it fun, but serious. Profit Producer. Productivity Expert. Creator of Great Ideas.

- **Print your own card.** Can't be any worse than the one you're carrying. Use both cards – one for image and one to prove creativity.

- **Bring a fun idea.** One that helps them.

- **Bring a fun book.** *Seuss-isms!* A small book about the big wisdom of Dr. Seuss.

- **Bring a short classic book.** A thought book. One that makes the CEO think about himself and thank you. *Acres of Diamonds* or *A Message to Garcia.* The best source for these books is www.executivebooks.com.

- **Write a compelling document on safety, their industry, productivity, or leadership.** This will take time and hard work; that's why most salespeople won't do it. But every CEO will appreciate it, and read it. Make sure you autograph it as you present it.

- **Bring an idea for improving or enhancing THEIR business.** This takes time, research, and creativity, but it will get you in the door – and keep you there.

CAUTION: One of the biggest and most fatal mistakes that salespeople make is "waiting" for someone else to give you sales tools. NO, that's not how great sales are made. That's not how you engage a CEO. Great impressions are made, great sales are made – and made often – with tools you give yourself.

Got tools?
Give them to yourself!

CHALLENGE 8
ACTIONS

MASTER CREATIVITY

- Buy, read, and study *Thinkertoys* by Michael Michalko. Best book on creativity in the 20th century. Edward de Bono's *Serious Creativity* is a close second.

- Understand that IDEAS are more powerful than slides. Bring ideas to meetings.

- Study creativity. It's a science; you can learn to be creative.

- Generate ideas every day. Some will actually be good!

- Ideas create a competitive advantage.

- Ideas start as thoughts and observation. PAY ATTENTION.

- Offer ideas in person if possible.

9
MASTER TIME

In the 1890s when Lewis Carroll wrote *Alice's Adventures in Wonderland*, he put an emphasis and a value on being on time.

You can see the images here from the 1890's original illustrated version of *Alice in Wonderland*. The rabbit talking to Alice says, "I'm late. I'm late, for a very important date, no time to say hello, goodbye. I'm late, I'm late." The chapter is entitled "Down a Rabbit Hole."

You have used a rabbit hole to waste time for years in this thing that we just had, this virus thing, whatever. You probably binge-watched stuff and blew hours of time away on television, when you could have been, should have been, *allocating* your time to something more productive, something more ingenious, something that would actually bring you revenue, build your reputation online, or be of value to your customers.

TIME CHALLENGE: Time is your most valuable asset. As we emerge into this New Normal time, *guard* your time, do not *spend* your time: *invest your time.* In my productivity book, *Get Sh*t Done*, which you should own and read and study, there's a life-changing quote by Orison Swett Marden: "People do not realize the immense value of utilizing spare minutes." That is from Marden's 1908 book, *He Can Who Thinks He Can.*

Okay, so I'm talking about spending time versus investing time. I think you can understand that concept right away. Let me define it further...

You've heard the expressions, "Get ready, get set, go" or "Ready, set, go!" The key is investing your time to *get ready* to *prepare.* In your preparation you put your mindset on self-confidence. When you get set, your self-talk says, "I can do this." Your attitude's right. THEN YOU GO. You don't go until you get ready and get set.

Me? I have a morning routine. I sit in my chair and I do five things. I read, I write, I prepare. That causes me to think and create and I've been doing that for 25 years. For an hour a day... **Read, Write, Prepare, Think, Create.**

The best way to get in the groove of a morning routine is to...

- **Create a quiet, creative space.** You have to have your own space.

- **Dedicate a specific time each day to YOU.** You, ready for your time.

- **Start your groove with something inspirational to read, listen to, or watch.**

- **Then move on to, and get into, your own thinking and doing.**

After a few days, you'll begin to understand the power of these you-on-you get-togethers. After a few weeks you'll be in the habit of doing it. After a few months you'll be in your own groove – thinking, reading, writing, and preparing to win for yourself. You're going to discover brand new ways of investing time and winning.

At some time during your journey, and you'll know when it is, it'll be time to post and venture into the virtual world of business. It's called virtual time, and your virtual time is going to set the tone for your long-term success. Not your flying in an airplane time, your virtual time. That means you're going to have more selling time.

What you're going to have to do is self-discipline yourself so that you have sober time. Hello, no beer, prep time or preparation time, study time, writing time. Literally preparing your time. My dad always said to me, son, you do your homework. Not in college but in life. He meant was I prepared for the meeting that I was going to have the following day, and I always did my homework. I did my homework, Pop. Sometimes I would call in advance and let him know that I'd done some amazing homework, and sometimes I actually got to show him my homework right in front of him.

Classic. Yeah.

CHALLENGE 9
ACTIONS

MASTER TIME

- Once again, Morning Routine plays a vital role in mastering this skill.

- Here are your orders... Create a quiet, creative space. Dedicate a specific time each morning to YOU. Start your groove with something inspirational to read, listen to, or watch, then move on to, and get into, your own thinking and doing. This SETS THE TONE for your daily productivity.

- Allocate your time; don't try to manage it.

- Do your homework. Get ready for your day the night before.

9.5
MASTER YOURSELF

I've just given you nine elements in the New Normal and new economy that I've challenged you to master. Go back and study every single one of them, but if you know me, you know I'm a .5 guy and this is 9.5 – Master Yourself.

LIVE. VIRTUAL. VIDEO.

These elements are NOT the new black – they're the new green. Money green.

I'm going to share a few words from the greatest speech ever given. Martin Luther King, Jr., from his immortal "I Have a Dream" speech. When MLK said "now is the time…" he was speaking then and now. Let me fast forward almost six decades and prove it's immortality and relevance to right now…

- *Now is the time* to emerge a winner and a leader.
- *Now is the time* to be your best for your family and friends.
- *Now is the time* to be your best for company and your customers.
- *Now is the time* to build your social platform and reputation.
- *Now is the time* to master virtual and video.
- *Now is the time* to master the new sales communication.
- *Now is the time* to master creativity and generate valuable ideas.
- *Now is the time* to START WITH YOURSELF.

To start mastering yourself, begin with loving yourself and believing in yourself. That's the mindset. And "Now is the time."

If you love yourself you have a chance to be your best self. My mantra has always been: Be the best you can be for yourself first; then and only then can you be the best you can be for others.

The great Jim Rohn said that formal education will earn you a living, but self-education will earn you a fortune. You decide how much money you want to earn by how much you decide you want to self-educate. It's just that simple. It's about investing in yourself. It's about being the best you can be for yourself. And *Now is the time.*

It's about capturing your selfish time, your attitude time, your reading time, your writing time, and make time work for you. NOW is YOUR time.

If you're going to emerge, you can emerge as anything you want in this time. It's a brand new time. Everything is changing. Virtual is changing. Video is changing. Writing is changing. Selling is changing. Be the leader, not the lagger. Don't sit in the pack of people and watch things emerge. Don't let this opportunity pass you by.

BEST WAY: Stop complaining about… I was home for three months. You know what? No one cares. Not one person cares that you ran out of toilet paper. What people care about is how you prepared yourself to emerge as a better person.

In August of 1963, Martin Luther King, Jr., delivered his immortal "I Have a Dream" speech in front of the Lincoln Memorial, addressing 500,000 people and the world. I personally consider that to be the most important and moving speech in America since the Gettysburg Address. In it King challenged his audience to take immediate action when he said, "Now is the time!"

I hope you're reading this or you're listening to this as the world is evolving post-pandemic of 2020 – even if it's 2030. I hope you're still open to doing what's now, new, and next… I hope you're still looking at what you can do for yourself, your family, your friends, and people you influence, your business, and your customers, and that you're inspired to react and respond to the command: Now is the time.

Now is the time!

Martin Luther King, Jr.

August 1963

CHALLENGE 9.5
ACTIONS

MASTER YOURSELF

- All good things start with YOU.
- Read, study, and implement *The Little Gold Book of YES! Attitude*.
- Start your day and your world with YES.
- You can't master anything or anyone until you have mastered yourself.
- You can't love anyone until you love yourself.

Framework for
GOING LIVE Success

Here's what you need, and what you need to do...

Visual Framework graphic – identify who you want to attend – create valuable content with ideas and information that people want – have a space and a setting that looks warm, comfortable, and professional – announce it with a flair both socially and personally to your connections – ask participants who join to share it – sell your wares after a month of two – never miss your appointed time – engage participants by asking them and responding to their answers. Be engaging. Be confident. Be accurate. Be valuable. Be funny. Be awesome.

HINT:
WATCH MY LIVE SHOW
Facebook.com/JeffreyGitomer
daily @ 9:59 a.m.
DO WHAT I DO

AUTHOR'S PERSONAL GO LIVE! SUCCESS CHALLENGE

This book would not be complete unless I told you to beware and be aware of how you take care of yourself. Emerge healthy. Don't abuse yourself. Keep yourself in perfect health. Relax. You're already at one with your family. Have you been happy with it? Take some personal time for yourself and your family. Create a routine each day that's tied to time.

Discover yourself, pay attention to yourself, and then you can begin to pay attention to everything that's around you. It's a matter of your concentration, your gratitude, your dedication to hard work, your power of observation, and your personal self-discipline.

You have to be happy on the inside and show thanks on the outside, thankful *to* people and thankful *for* people, thankful for your friendships, thankful for things, and honor the people or kids who are thankful for your fatherhood, or your motherhood.

JEFFREY GITOMER'S INSIDER'S CLUB

OWN AND MASTER
The New Normal Course by joining my exclusive Insider's Club

I've given you the mastery for what you have to do in order to be able to Go Live! and emerge as a winner. But that's just the beginning. My Insider's Club will keep you winning and introduce you to other winners from all over the world.

Gitomer.com/InsidersClub will help you get from here to wherever you want to go. It's limitless, or it's only limited by the amount of time and a few dollars that you invest in the most important person in the world. You.

If you liked the book, you'll LOVE the Insider's Club. The url will get you all the details. Take a look.

JEFFREY GITOMER
King of Sales

Gitomer Defined (git-o-mer) n. 1. a creative, on-the-edge writer and speaker whose expertise on sales, customer loyalty, and personal development is world-renowned; **2.** known for presentations, seminars, and keynote addresses that are funny, insightful, and in-your-face; **3.** real-world; **4.** off-the-wall; **5.** on the money; and **6.** give audiences information they can take out in the street one minute after the seminar is over and then they can turn it into money. He is the ruling King of Sales.

See also: salesman.

AUTHOR. Jeffrey Gitomer is the author of the *New York Times* bestsellers *The Sales Bible, The Little Red Book of Selling, The Little Black Book of Connections,* and *The Little Gold Book of YES! Attitude.* Most of his books have been number one bestsellers on Amazon.com, including *Customer Satisfaction Is Worthless, Customer Loyalty Is Priceless, The Patterson Principles of Selling, The Little Red Book of Sales Answers, The Little Green Book of Getting Your Way, The Little Platinum Book of Cha-Ching!, The Little Teal Book of Trust, Social BOOM!, The Little Book of Leadership,* the *21.5 Unbreakable Laws of Selling,* and the *Sales Manifesto.* Jeffrey's books have appeared on major bestseller lists more than 500 times and have sold millions of copies worldwide.

OVER 75 PRESENTATIONS A YEAR. Jeffrey gives public and corporate seminars, runs annual sales meetings, and conducts live and virtual training programs on selling, YES! Attitude, trust, customer loyalty, and personal development.

AWARD FOR PRESENTATION EXCELLENCE. In 1997, Jeffrey was awarded the designation of Certified Speaking Professional (CSP) by the National Speakers Association. The CSP award has been given fewer than 500 times in the past 25 years and is the association's highest earned designation.

SPEAKER HALL OF FAME. In August 2008, Jeffrey was inducted into the National Speakers Association's Speaker Hall of Fame. The designation CPAE (Counsel of Peers Award for Excellence) honors professional speakers who have reached the top echelon of performance excellence. Each candidate must demonstrate mastery in seven categories: originality of material, uniqueness of style, experience, delivery, image, professionalism, and communication. To date, 191 of the world's greatest speakers have been inducted, including Ronald Reagan, Art Linkletter, Colin Powell, Norman Vincent Peale, Earl Nightingale, and Zig Ziglar.

BUSINESS SOCIAL MEDIA.

@JEFFREYGITOMER

ONLINE SALES AND PERSONAL DEVELOPMENT TRAINING.
Gitomer Learning Academy is all Jeffrey, all the time. It contains
Jeffrey's real-world practical sales information, strategies, and
ideas that starts with a skills-based assessment and then offers an
interactive certification course. It's ongoing sales motivation and
reinforcement with the ability to track, measure, and monitor
progress and achievement. Go to GitomerLearningAcademy.com.

SALES CAFFEINE. Jeffrey's free weekly newsletter, *Sales Caffeine*,
is a wake-up call delivered every Tuesday morning to more than
250,000 subscribers. You can subscribe at www.gitomer.com/
sales-caffeine.

SELL OR DIE PODCAST. Jeffrey Gitomer and Jennifer Gluckow
share their sales and personal development knowledge in their
podcast, *Sell or Die*. In today's world of constant change there is
still one constant, you're either selling or dying. Tune in on iTunes
or your favorite podcast app – just search for *Sell or Die*.

The evolution of video has become the revolution of video.
Going Live is no longer optional.
It's essential.

Jeffrey Gitomer